Buying Your VACATION HOME *for Fun & Profit*

Ruth Rejnis
Claire Walter

D1445498

**Real Estate
Education Company**
a division of Dearborn Financial Publishing, Inc.

This publication is designed to provide accurate and authoritative information in regard to the subject matter covered. It is sold with the understanding that the publisher is not engaged in rendering legal, accounting or other professional service. If legal advice or other expert assistance is required, the services of a competent professional person should be sought.

Acquisitions Editor: Christine E. Litavsky
Managing Editor: Jack Kiburz
Interior Design: Lucy Jenkins
Cover Design: ST & Associates
Typesetting: Elizabeth Pitts

Published by Real Estate Education Company®,
a division of Dearborn Financial Publishing, Inc.®

Printed in the United States of America

96 97 98 10 9 8 7 6 5 4 3 2 1

Library of Congress Cataloging-in-Publication Data

Rejnis, Ruth.
    Buying your vacation home for fun and profit / by Ruth Rejnis and
Claire Walter.
        p.   cm.
    Includes index.
    ISBN 0-7931-1583-3 (pbk.)
    1. Vacation homes—United States—Purchasing. 2. Second homes—
United States—Purchasing. 3. Real estate investment—United
States. I. Walter, Claire. II. Title.
HD7289.3.U6R45   1996
643'.2—dc20   96-23242
                                                      CIP

Real Estate Education Company books are available at special quantity discounts to use as premiums and sales promotions, or for use in corporate training programs. For more information, please call the Special Sales Manager at 800-621-9621, ext. 4384, or write to Dearborn Financial Publishing, Inc., 155 N. Wacker Drive, Chicago, IL 60606-1719.

DEDICATION

With the hope that you, the reader, will find your own idyllic get-away, to enjoy for many years to come

CONTENTS

PART THREE
What's In and What's Not:
A Look at Popular Second-Home Destinations

PART FOUR
The ABCs of Purchasing and Profiting from Your Home

PART ONE

Considering a Weekend (or Longer) Getaway

CHAPTER 1

Vacation Homes Are Today's Hot Ticket

Beach house, country place, weekend getaway, lakeside cabin, ski condo, resort timeshare, apartment abroad—they have a nice ring to them, don't they? Wouldn't you like to use one in the context of *your* life? Perhaps in reading this list you already know which type of second home would be *your* escape from it all.

WHY SO MANY WANT A GETAWAY

A 1995 survey by the American Resort Development Association, a Washington, D.C.–based trade group, found that 35 percent of households feel they have a better-than-even chance of purchasing recreational property in the next ten years, a figure that is up from 26 percent in 1993 and 16 percent in 1990.

It is not hard to see why we want such an escape. If our lives are hectic and harried—and few of us would say we have no stresses—we desire a spot, however modest, where we can head for weekends or a few times a year to relax, regroup, gain some perspective, and occasionally, lick our wounds and gear up for the week or season to come.

Home is a wonderful place. Home is, well, where the heart is. But home is familiar, too. A vacation home has an edge of familiarity, but not being there every day also makes each visit somewhat new.

Ever notice how nicely some people—including kids—get along in fresh, new surroundings? There's something about a second home that changes most of us when we are there. For one thing, being there offers the opportunity to shed the day-to-day routine and explore. Of course, there may be geographic explorations such as driving, walking, horseback riding or boating around your part-time locale, or always something different to admire or learn. There is also the *new you* that seems to be "born" from a second home.

This new you is willing to try ice skating for the first time since you were 15. The vacationing-you might start building some furniture, projects in your mind for years that have never seen the light of day. The part-time-you finally has time to smell the roses—and becomes so entranced that it leads to an absorbing new hobby growing them at that vacation spot.

Or you can flip in the opposite direction: The vacation-you, usually a nonstop dynamo back home, is in this setting the hammock-swinging-you.

With a vacation home, you also have the choice of getting away alone with the family, sharing time that can be far more "quality" than those busy days back home. You can also invite houseguests to your place for weekends, or weeks, to get caught up with your extended family and close friends.

Those with a second home seem delighted with their good fortune, as you will see when you read their stories throughout this book.

Ah, leisure and travel, what a combo. *Numbers News,* a demographics newsletter, reported in a 1995 issue that 44 percent of adults claim that owning a second home is essential to the good life. That figure is up 18 percentage points since 1984.

Did You Know . . .

. . . that the first house built for summer use only in this country was in New Hampshire. It was constructed in 1769 for John Wentworth, the last royal governor of that state. It stood on 4,000 acres in Wolfeboro, on the shores of Lake Wentworth.

Source: *The Old Farmer's Almanac*

PRACTICALLY SPEAKING

A growing number of Americans want a second home for another reason besides pleasure: a second home can be a good investment. A well-placed house or condominium in a vacation setting is almost certain to be of value because mountains, oceans or rivers are limited resources. There is potential rental income to think about, too, if you choose to make your investment work for you while you are back home.

Yes, you may find better investments than a vacation home, outlets for your money that will earn more for your initial investment dollar. There are expenses to owning a vacation home, but there are also some tax savings.

With an initial outlay of money from you in the form of a down payment, a second home can bring you many enjoyable years of holidays, and then a profit when you eventually sell. Of course, your place could be so much fun and so perfect for your needs and interests that you never do sell. In fact, it might become an important part of your estate and be handed down for generations.

DEFINITION, PLEASE

It's pretty obvious what a vacation home is, isn't it? It's . . . on reflection, perhaps a definition *is* needed. A vacation place is a second home used by the owner only occasionally and is not the principal or voting residence. The vacation-home buyer can either rent or own his or her primary residence.

Usually the second home is in a resort setting—near a lake, river or ocean—although it can be out in the country among year-round homes, too. Most buyers choose a place they can visit on weekends without too much effort or not too distant from their primary homes.

It's interesting that even though a second home can be in the city, it is not thought of as a second home in common usage. If suburban or country dwellers want to buy a place downtown for staying late after work, to attend city cultural events or to pop down for a weekend of shopping, it's usually known as a *pied-à-terre*, or "our apartment in town." However, the Internal Revenue Service certainly considers it a vacation home if that is how the owners designate it and they have another, permanent residence.

Also, for a property to be considered a vacation home as it is used in the context of this book, you have to stay there some of the time. If you buy a condominium in the Caribbean, rent it and watch it appreciate (you hope) but never stay there, you have an investment property, not a true vacation home. It's there for someone else's vacation.

Otherwise, wherever you choose, your sometimes escape can be a vacation home. It might be a single-family house, a two-family dwelling, a condominium, town house, patio home or, as you will see in these pages, a recreational vehicle or boat. Maybe your getaway is a one-week timeshare in a resort 200 miles from your home. You might own your second home with some friends. All of these housing and ownership styles are considered in these pages.

GET 'EM WHILE THEY'RE HOT— AND THERE ARE SOME LEFT

This is a good time to buy a vacation home. Prices have been down for a few years now. Couple that with the onset of a great demand for those properties and you have a window of opportunity that should allow you to buy quite nicely.

Signs of the onset of a great demand:

- A growing number of Europeans have been purchasing vacation properties in some regions here, naturally competing for those homes with American buyers.
- More and more Americans have been buying into vacation communities to live there full time. They can be retirees, telecommuters and those willing to put in a long daily commute to live in a resort, either because they like that setting or some homes are more affordable there. Of course that trend reduces the number of existing properties likely to come on the market in those towns.
- The baby boomers are coming—a cry you have probably heard often these days.The prime group buying vacation property comprises folks in their 40s and early 50s with older children or perhaps kids already out of the house. Or no kids at all. There are some 80.5 million baby boomers (in an overall American population of 260.3 million). They have developers and real estate agents grinning about the coming years of second-home buying, but they could soon cause a mad scrambling for resort properties. The second largest major group buying vacation property is made up of Americans between 55 and 64.
- Environmental controls in scenic and resort communities have led to the squelching of new building and the creation of land

---

What's a "Boomer"? What's a "Yup"?

Baby boomers are those Americans born between 1946 and 1964. They are often in the news these days because of their sizable numbers and because, with the oldest turning 50, Congress has been nervously considering their upcoming needs for Social Security, Medicare and other government services. Private companies and services are also looking at that huge market. "Yups" or "yuppies" is a casual term that stands for young urban professionals—folks in their 20s and 30s living in the big city—and referred to by some oldsters as "!*%@!!* yuppies."

---

banks. Because many residents of these communities want to stop further growth, politicians acquiesce by enacting controls. The result is that one day you might not be able to buy or build where you'd like.

- Finally, there is the product—the resort area—itself. Only so many oceanfront communities, for example, are available, and most of them are already built to capacity. Many desirable resort areas are filling fast, leaving it to builders to discover new ones where they might run into no-growth controls and restrictions. We have plenty of land in this country, but not an inexhaustible supply of resort areas.

IT IS NOT THAT DIFFICULT TO BUY THESE DAYS

We think these are good times to buy because the market has been slow in recent years but preparing for a major takeoff. Couple a slow market with today's reasonable mortgage interest rates, and, from a financial standpoint, this is a good time to buy. With the variety of properties we consider in this book, you can probably buy *some* getaway if you want one and be a very happy second-home owner quite soon.

We'll help you with the selection and buying process throughout this book.

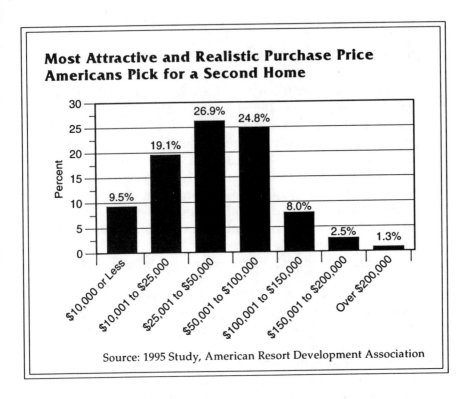

Most Attractive and Realistic Purchase Price Americans Pick for a Second Home

Source: 1995 Study, American Resort Development Association

KEEP IN MIND

➤ Your vacation home can be anywhere that is not considered your principal residence.

➤ Second-home sales are now picking up after some slow years.

➤ The mortgage picture looks good right now too.

➤ State and/or local environmental restrictions on vacation land use, plus the push by residents of many resort communities for slow, or no, growth, could put a crimp in your buying plans now and certainly in the future.

CHAPTER 2

Determining Your Vacation Style

"From the mountains to the prairies, to the oceans white with foam," ours is a huge and varied country from which to select a second home. Let's not forget the lakefronts and the deserts. And for the adventurous, perhaps a vacation home in a foreign country.

Which of the above sounds like you? Here are some quizzes, which should be both fun and practical. They will help crystallize your interests and holiday objectives so that you can pinpoint the vacation home that will bring you the most pleasure.

There are, of course, no right or wrong answers. How and where you prefer to spend your leisure time is not a science. It is emotional even though plenty of common sense and rational thinking should also enter a picture where thousands of dollars are involved. You will notice that throughout these pages when we talk of the magic of vacation homes and use the "sun-setting-on-crystal-blue-waters" type of prose, we also consider the practical side. Your second home might be a dream come true, but you have to pay for it with a very real mortgage or very real green dollars.

Have a pencil and pad ready? Jot down your answers to the following questions, and then read the explanation that follows each set.

THE SEASONAL-YOU

Let's narrow down the season you should aim for with your vacation home. If possible, your property should be where your favorite time of year is high season:

- Do you prefer summer vacations, whether because you like the warm weather or because the kids are out of school and it is just easier to get away then?
- Are you strictly a cold-weather type? Do you want to leave a resort when the snow starts melting?
- Do you look for *everything* in a second home—good winter activities and something to do during the other seasons as well?

Naturally, if you have kids' school schedules to consider, you'll have more flexibility and more time to spend at a summer resort. If you prefer summer getaways anyway, then good—it all works out rather effortlessly. Head for the beach—lake or bay or oceanfront—or for the desert, where you can soak up all that warmth, wearing the appropriate sun block, of course.

If, on the other hand, you are a cold-weather enthusiast, then a mountain or skiing community, or any other spot where winter is the high season with all of the activities and special programs that brings, will make you happiest. Incidentally, you don't have to ski in a ski town—there's plenty to do off the slopes if you just enjoy cold air, snow and the ambience of a winter resort.

If you want to get away any time of the year, whenever you can snatch a few days or weeks, you might make the winter choice. Many mountain and ski resorts are yearlong now, allowing you plenty to do—and see—in what was once off-season. A home in the country offers another choice. It will be attractive and busy (for the country) in spring, summer and fall; your only concern could be the dead of winter when you might not want to visit anyway.

A lakefront or oceanside, and exclusively resort, community in the northern part of the East Coast, for example, probably would not work for the all-season you. It might be dreary in the winter and not that lively in the spring or autumn either unless you like a quiet life mingling only with permanent residents in the downtime. With more and more retirees living in resort areas full time, however, the town you favor just might not be so dreary in the off-season.

Here's another option for the all-season second-home shopper: a timeshare or condominium, or even a rental apartment, in the nearest major urban center where there is always plenty to do all year.

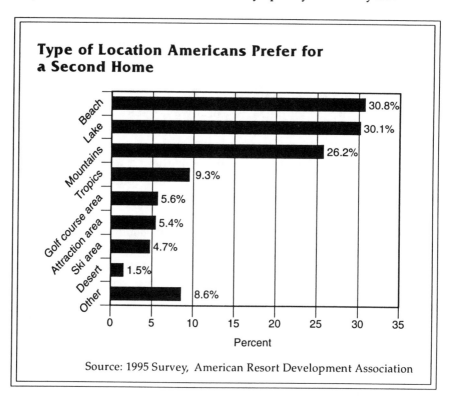

Type of Location Americans Prefer for a Second Home

Location	Percent
Beach	30.8%
Lake	30.1%
Mountains	26.2%
Tropics	9.3%
Golf course area	5.6%
Attraction area	5.4%
Ski area	4.7%
Desert	1.5%
Other	8.6%

Source: 1995 Survey, American Resort Development Association

HOW DO YOU LIKE TO SPEND YOUR LEISURE TIME?

Your interests will have a great deal to do with the vacation property you choose. With this next set of questions, just jot down some notes after answering, such as "fishing important" or "last two vacations were at beach."

When you first thought about a vacation home while reading this book, perhaps when you saw the title, did you immediately envision a particular vacation home? What was it: a ski house? a condo on a golf course? a community near you on a lake? Your initial response might be the best choice for you.

How did you spend your last vacation? No, not the one when you re-painted the house; the one before that when you left town for a few days or weeks? And the year before that? Is there a pattern emerging? Do you always head for the beach? Do you drive or fly to the nearest big city for a culture fix?

This is important to take into account: Did you go to a particular spot because you wanted to or because you were expected to by family or because of other considerations? If you didn't want to be there, don't count it in profiling your interests.

Another point to ponder: Do you always seem to head for your folks' place—or your spouse's or companion's parents' home—maybe 60 miles, or 600 miles, from your place? Perhaps you genuinely like vis-iting family and friends you have there. Is there a resort area nearby that you might consider for a second home? You could have your own place when you visit family and perhaps entertain them and your friends while there.

Is there a particular sport you must engage in on holiday? More than one: golf, swimming, hiking, skiing, walking, boating, horseback riding?

Is there any one particular non-sports-related leisure activity vital to your enjoying a vacation, such as sightseeing, sunbathing, shopping, casino gambling?

Do you like to keep busy on holiday, or do you want to "veg out"?

Do you prefer to rough it, or are you strictly a room-service-at-the-Regency type?

Do you have a current passport that has been stamped several times over the last few years?

Now looking over your scribbled comments, you can pretty much tell where your interests lie and what type of setting will make you happiest.

For example, if you don't like to engage in too much physical activ-ity on a holiday, but you do like sightseeing and you're the room-ser-vice sort, you're not going to be happy in the country with nothing to "sightsee" but trees, trees and more trees, and perhaps an interstate. A full-service condominium resort might be your speed. Or a city apart-ment.

If sports are important to you, consider a vacation setting that will allow you to participate in sports you like. That might be a single-fam-ily home in a community with many opportunities for fishing, golf, and so on or owning a condo or timeshare in a resort featuring many sporting activities.

Do you like a good deal of sightseeing and *really* enjoy roughing it? You might consider a recreational vehicle, which will allow you to always see something new and even cook out-of-doors if you choose. If you always seem to gravitate to waterfront vacations, think about a house along a lake, ocean or river, although you might also want to get *on* that water and make a boat your second home.

Finally, about that passport question. If you have traveled out of the country a few times over the years, you might enjoy a second home abroad. The place you buy abroad could be even more affordable than one in this country, as you will see in Chapter 9.

This has been a mix-and-match section. You will have to take your answers, line them up and then, as we have done in the above paragraphs, figure out the vacation style that is really you. There is no blueprint to conform to—it's your own interests and preferences that matter.

The "you" that we use throughout this chapter includes both couples and individuals. A couple will naturally have to take each other's tastes and choices into consideration when choosing a second home. Compromise might be necessary, but the decision is too important for one of you to make too many, or all, of the concessions. You should both be pleased—yes, even excited—about the decision to buy and the new lifestyle it affords.

Did You Know. . .

. . . that a vacation home should be purchased for recreation and personal enjoyment first, then for such other benefits as appreciation of the property?

LET'S TALK ABOUT TIME AND DISTANCE . . .

The next thing to consider is the amount of time you hope to spend at your vacation place. Are you planning to head for that spot

- every weekend?
- just a month during the high season?
- a few times over the course of a year at different seasons?

If you want to get in your car on Friday at 5 o'clock many times throughout the year and head for your second home, look for a resort area within a distance comfortable for you. Then you won't decide after two or three weekends that the whole idea is totally impractical. If you rarely visit for a weekend because of the unreasonable distance, much of the enjoyment of your second home is gone. *You* will have to determine how many hours of driving is reasonable. Some will say two or three hours on a Friday, tops. Others can push farther.

Pegi and Jay Adam carefully calculated the distance from their New York year-round residence to their New England ski place.

"We have a condo at Mt. Snow, in Vermont," Pegi Adam, who works in Manhattan, explains. "It takes us 4½ hours to get there, and we go every weekend during the ski season. That's the reason we chose Mt. Snow—it's the shortest trip. If we had gone to Killington, it would be five hours or more." Every half hour counts on Friday night.

The Adam family chose 4½ hours as their driving limit. You might get out the old atlas and draw a circle around areas as many miles from home as you are willing to drive. The resort communities that fall within that circle should be a relatively easy commute for frequent weekend visits.

If you have children younger than their teens, you might want to give some thought—perhaps plenty of thought—to how well they will travel on frequent weekend trips. That could affect how far you are willing to go. The Adam family eventually figured out the easiest way to drive from one home to another for their two young boys.

"We got a van," says Pegi Adam, "so each kid has his own seat. They have hookups for electronic things, too, although there's no television. Each kid has a laptop." They seem to be entertained quite nicely during the trip to Mt. Snow.

If you plan to visit your home just once or twice a year, then distance does not play that great a role in your choice. You can go far afield if you like. However, you may have to consider plane fares to your destination and the extra responsibility of renting and maintaining the place by long distance.

. . . AND, OF COURSE, MONEY

Did we mention you will have to pay for your vacation-home dream? But the good news, as we have mentioned and will continue to discuss, is that there is a vacation home for almost every pocketbook.

When Renting Is Uppermost In Your Mind

The best choice if you are looking for as much income as possible is an all-season home, one that will offer the most opportunities for renting out throughout the year. And even if you don't plan to rent your vacation home, you may still want a getaway with year-round attractions.

You can almost certainly have your getaway and one at or near the activities you want. That home will be yours to enjoy now and for many years ahead.

Are you a little bit clearer now about what you will be looking for in a vacation home? Although pinpointing what you want is certainly a sensible, time-saving proposition, you would still be wise to read all of the possibilities in this book. Just like romance, sometimes a vacation style you hadn't given a moment's thought to materializes unexpectedly, and the next thing you know, it's a perfect match.

KEEP IN MIND

➤ Every resort area isn't for every personality or temperament. Look for the one where you will feel most comfortable.

➤ If you want to use your second home on weekends, decide on the time you are willing to spend driving to and from that spot on Friday and Sunday evenings (or Monday mornings), and choose a resort area accordingly.

➤ Don't make too many sacrifices in choosing what you want from a vacation home. This is holiday time, after all, and you should be able to feed some of those getting-away-from-it-all fantasies of yours.

PART TWO

Your Many Housing Options

CHAPTER 3

House? Condo?
What's Your Pleasure?

Let's continue exploring your vacation-home style: this time the dwelling itself. What form will the roof over your head take? Not literally, as in gabled or tar or red tile, but figuratively, as in the type of home you think you would like to buy.

In later chapters we consider recreational vehicles and boats as well as buying land or an island or a timeshare apartment.

Here we will talk about two popular second-home choices—the single-family house and the condominium.

AND THE WINNER IS . . .

As you will see from the chart, most Americans prefer a single-family house (or a cabin) for a second home. That type of dwelling offers

- privacy;
- space;
- room to putter outdoors if you want to dip into landscaping or gardening; and
- familiarity.

A second home might be similar to your principal residence, making a comfortable segue into a second-home purchase. Having listed the

19

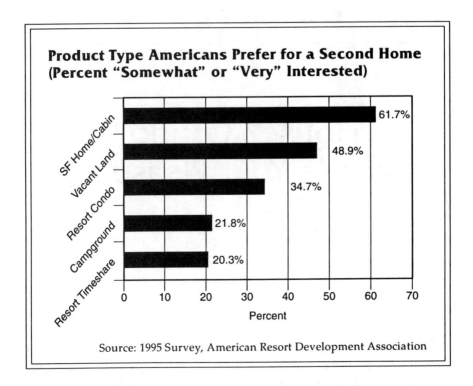

Product Type Americans Prefer for a Second Home (Percent "Somewhat" or "Very" Interested)

- SF Home/Cabin: 61.7%
- Vacant Land: 48.9%
- Resort Condo: 34.7%
- Campground: 21.8%
- Resort Timeshare: 20.3%

Percent

Source: 1995 Survey, American Resort Development Association

advantages of a house, we can ask: are there any drawbacks? Yes, if you are still undecided which type of home you want. Here are a few drawbacks you should note:

- With a house you will have to repair the leaky roof, keep up the front of the house and lawn, and in general have the same repair and maintenance responsibilities you have with your principal home.
- If you rent your property for a time when you are not there, your tenant will have to keep up with that lawn and/or snow removal, or you will have to pay an outside service.
- There is the responsibility, too, of closing up the house for what might be many months before you, or tenants, return again. You might worry about your property from your principal home when you hear, or read about, storms, floods, hurricanes and the like. You might also worry about breaking and entering.

Getting back to the positives if a house is your preference, you can see from the chart that single-family houses rate first with many others, too. If the locale is wisely chosen, you should have a good investment and no trouble selling when you want. You have gone with a popular choice.

THE CONDOMINIUM, PLAIN AND FANCY

It's easy to see why many vacationers opt for a condominium—a condo—as a second home:

- They can be less expensive than a single-family home.
- The space—exterior and interior—is manageable.
- Frequently a condo is purchased completely furnished.
- Outside maintenance is taken care of by the condo association.
- You can feel relatively protected from break-ins when you are not there.
- While some condo communities contain just a few units and maybe some parking spaces, others consist of a hundred or more apartments, with many amenities, such as swimming pools, tennis courts, riding trails, a golf course and on and on.
- Some resort condos will help you rent your unit when you are not there.
- Some will help you sell, too, if and when you want.

Are there any drawbacks to this vacation ownership style? A few, of course, or we would all be in condominiums:

- A condominium involves communal living. You own your unit from the interior walls in. The exterior walls and all of the common areas you own jointly with other owners and you must pay a monthly maintenance fee that covers property taxes for the common areas, office staff salaries, upkeep of the grounds and the like. With this housing style you are indeed tied to your neighbor.

    For the good of the community or, more correctly, for the good of property values, a lengthy list details what you can and cannot do with your condo, such as paint it a color different from the others, plop a satellite dish on the front lawn or hang laundry outdoors; these are but a few examples of many restrictions. Some buyers like these rules and regulations, whereas others resent them. If you think you fit into the latter category, then you would probably be happier with a home that is not part of a community association.

- Monthly maintenance fees do tend to rise, sometimes every year. That escalation could eventually become a financial burden to you.
- A condo might be too small for you if you have a large family and plan to do a good deal of entertaining, and neighbors might complain about noise as well.

Brrrrr . . . But Cute

How small can a vacation getaway be? We mean a house, not an RV. How about 10 × 20 feet, perhaps even tinier? That is the common size for an ice-fishing house, a not unusual "second home" in some northern states. Some of these houses are furnished around one or up to ten ice holes. Others are quite snappy and even become summer homes (they are towed to a lot on land before the three feet of ice that serves as a foundation begins to melt). Ice houses can cost from around $6,000 to whatever the owners want to spend for the home and decor.

The Tony Townhome

Townhomes are an architectural choice. They are two- or three-story individual units of attached housing operating under the condominium form of ownership. The townhome community appears the same as a condo complex, only taller. Sometimes, however, a townhome developer opts for the look of a single-family home, even an estate, rather than a row of attached homes. Each of several buildings, with a few apartments inside, might have a steeply pitched, or a turret-shaped, roof supported by white columns, giving the appearance of a "manor" home.

Technically, townhomes can also be single-family houses built in a row, perhaps called townhouses. They are individually owned like any house on private land, and they can have or not have an owners association and common area. This single-family style of townhouse is often found downtown, of course, and sometimes in a brand-new community that is trying to offer, whether for style's sake or because of lack of land on which to build, the look of a town with sidewalks and streetlights.

Townhomes do not always offer more square footage than a one-story condo apartment, and they can come with quite affordable price tags as well as being very highly priced.

Something Special: The Resort Condo

You can find, in almost any vacation area, nice, small condominium buildings or complexes that offer few amenities as well as those with a pool and tennis courts. Here we look at a resort with seemingly every-thing—lavish landscaping, attractive buildings, amenities galore—and more. Maybe a conference center is on the site and/or a major enter-tainment arena with a theater.

At these resorts you have a choice of fully furnished condo apart-ments, from efficiencies to one-, two- or three-bedroom units. There is daily housekeeping service, probably a restaurant and lounge, a health club, outdoor and perhaps indoor pool(s) and whirlpool spa, valet ser-vice, tennis courts, riding trails, kids' activities, golfing and whatever else can be tossed in to make you divinely happy during your vacation. If you need a spot to dock your boat, that will likely be available. If on-site day care will make your holiday blissful, some resorts will provide that.

Another advantage of these top-of-the-line communities: Many have programs allowing their owners to trade with other resorts around the country and around the world, so they can vary their vaca-tion settings if they choose.

Prices at these communities, which are likely to be found in prime resort areas, run the gamut, depending on many factors: the part of the country, whether the resort complex is old or new, how hot (popular-ity, not weather) the resort town is, the size and location of the unit for sale, and the laundry list of amenities. If we say you can pay under $75,000 for a unit or well over $1 million, that is an accurate range, con-sidering the many differences between resorts from coast to coast.

Whatever your condo costs at a fancy resort, you can also expect to pay a monthly maintenance fee that can run from around $200 to well over $500. Extra services, such as entering the community's rental pro-gram or having the resort sell your unit if it handles sales, will cost you extra, of course.

Got a Quarter?

Most vacation-home hunters pay for their units outright and have access to them year-round, both in and out of season. But a home style known as "quarter ownership" was introduced with little fanfare several years ago in a few major resort areas. If you didn't want a whole place or could not afford one, at least not one as fancy as you would have liked, you could purchase a one-quarter ownership, or equity stake, in a single-family house or condominium. Developers considered this buying style a response to the sometimes high prices of homes in prime resort areas. If buyers couldn't swing a $250,000 condo, they reasoned, maybe they would be willing to pay $65,000, and be able to spend 13 weeks at that home each year.

These homes are fully furnished and equipped condos, and are not to be confused with timeshares, where you buy only vacation time. Unlike timeshares, quarter ownership is very much a real estate purchase. Each family has its own deed and mortgage, and pays its own upkeep expenses.

The four buyers determine when they will use the property, and that time is written into a contract. Weeks that are most desired, such as holiday periods, can be rotated annually.

An owners association or management company is involved to oversee the operation of the property and develop the bylaws. That company also acts as an intermediary in cases of default or other conflicts. Buyers pay an annual maintenance fee covering these services and other expenses.

Quarter-ownership homes—and some selling 10 percent ownership—can still be found in prime vacation communities. With the demand for second homes heating up and likely to stay high, this buying style could make a more high-profile reappearance one of these days.

Of course, buying a portion of a house has always been around informally as family members or friends band together to purchase a house or condo.

FOR MORE INFORMATION

If you are condominium shopping, contact the attorney general's office in the state where you plan to buy for their printed materials on what to look for—and watch out for—when buying a condo. Many states offer this consumer information.

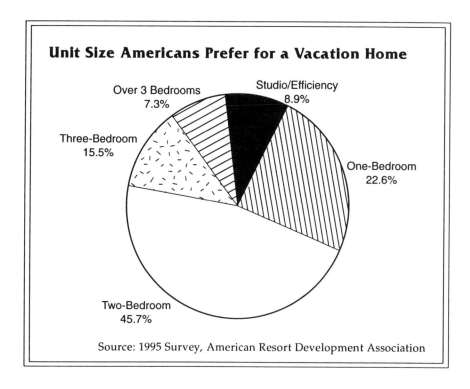

Unit Size Americans Prefer for a Vacation Home

Over 3 Bedrooms
7.3%

Studio/Efficiency
8.9%

Three-Bedroom
15.5%

One-Bedroom
22.6%

Two-Bedroom
45.7%

Source: 1995 Survey, American Resort Development Association

KEEP IN MIND

➤ The single-family house is the first choice of most second-home shoppers. If wisely chosen, it can be an excellent real estate investment for you.

➤ Condominiums in vacation areas come in all price ranges and styles, such as high-rise buildings, garden complexes and townhomes.

➤ The full-service resort condominium can offer a totally care-free holiday with recreational facilities galore. It can cost a bit, but you might find that luxury worth the money.

CHAPTER 4

Swap and Try It Before You Buy It

You're *pretty* sure you like Lakeview and want to buy there, but staying in a motel for two or three weeks on vacation . . . well, is that any indication of daily life in that town?

No, it isn't. You would have to live like the residents to see what's really what in Lakeview. That would include reading the daily paper, having breakfast in a local coffee shop, dealing with service people and talking to neighbors, especially about local concerns and issues. You would have to live in an apartment or house in that community for a while too.

Renting can be expensive, but there is a way of settling in for a short period that will cost you nothing, or perhaps just $60 or so. Swap your home for someone's in, or very close to, Lakeview.

"OH, HOME SWAPPING"

You have probably read about this vacation style over the last several years, probably because it has become increasingly popular as more people become familiar with the concept—and as travel and vacation costs continue to escalate. The concept is quite simple: You trade your three-bedroom city house for someone's apartment or house in a place you'd like to visit, either in this country or abroad, for an agreed-upon length of time.

This is not an idea likely to appeal to everyone. If you worry about strangers using your house, you will never relax and enjoy your vacation in their home. It takes a certain spirit to enjoy swapped holidays, the kind of attitude that where you go and what you see is more important than household possessions. (And, after all, you can put away very valuable items before you leave home.)

The concept of house swapping took root in the 1960s, when a New York schoolteacher started the first swap service intended primarily for teachers, who could not usually afford expensive hotel or motel charges. Today the Vacation Exchange Club—there's more about them coming up in the next few pages—is the largest of the home-swap organizations.

You can find an individual or family to trade with you by running a classified advertisement in the daily paper of the city or small town you'd like to visit. You can exchange letters with the respondents, perhaps phone calls as well.

An easier way, though, is to join one of the nation's home-swap clubs, which print directories of like-minded members. Then members work out the exchange between themselves.

The club directories offer page after page of entries. Each trader has a few lines indicating name and address, the family's accommodations, location, number of bedrooms and the like, whether there are pets and, finally, where and when that homeowner or renter would like to go for a holiday. Members interested in a listing write directly to the homeowner to make a match. In the same vein, when you receive your copy of the members' directory, you pore over it until you find a house or perhaps several homes in different areas that appeal to you. Then *you* write. Many listings include photographs of the owners' homes, which can range from quite lavish to very simple. There is no need to feel your home is too modest for this type of vacation.

The key to a successful swap, say those who run the organizations and the traders themselves, is being flexible. Bill and Mary Barbour, who live on Florida's west coast, have made 82 trades since their retirement in 1983, vacationing from Hong Kong through South Africa to Cape Cod, and many ports and inland communities in between. Bill Barbour has since written about home swaps—more about that at the end of the chapter.

"It's important not to limit yourself to where you are willing to go," he says. "For example, don't say you want Sanibel Island only; say you want the west coast of Florida." Flexibility will bring you more swap options during the weeks you want. And the distance from one community to another is not so great that you can't visit your first choice when you are on vacation.

For your purpose as a potential second-home buyer, being in the next town can still give you a good idea of daily life if you can't work out a match with your first choice, and you don't want to wait another year to vacation in that area.

Sizzle, Sizzle

What's a hot spot for home trades? Bill Barbour says he has been seeing an unusual amount of interest in Santa Fe, New Mexico. "It has a lot of luster," he says. One couple, he noted, traded their home for a place in Santa Fe and liked the area so much that they purchased a lot and had a home built right next door to the home they were swapping.

"TELL ME MORE," YOU SAY

Karl Costabel, the owner of the now 16,000-member Vacation Exchange Club, says, "If there's a common thread running through the membership in a home-swap club, it's that everyone's easygoing." And, Costabel adds, very interested in travel but often without the funds to see as much of the world as they would like if they had to spend vacation time and money on hotels and restaurant meals.

"I find a lot of people get into this to save money," Costabel points out, "but they stay in because they enjoy the people they're meeting and the way they're living where they vacation."

You, of course, will not only be vacationing in your traded home but also looking perhaps to buy in that community. This is more serious business for you, and you will no doubt keep your eyes open and mentally process every detail you observe in that community for placing in either your "town good for buying" file or the "skip this one" folder.

You're sold, but you say you don't live in a place anyone would want to visit. There's very little tourism in Upper Succotash, you point out.

You'd be surprised who would want to stay in your home. Perhaps it's someone who grew up in that town and wants to come back to visit family or for a special occasion, such as a wedding or a high school reunion. A retired couple who moved to the Sun Belt might want to come back home to visit their children and grandchildren, and they prefer the comfort—and quiet—of their own place.

"Sometimes people want to be in or near a college town," Bill Barbour explains, "to visit their child or grandchild. There's also business travel. I know a guy in Minnesota who goes to New York City every year with his wife on business, and swaps with someone who goes to *his* home in Minneapolis."

These days just about every place is near some city or town of note or some tourist attractions. You just never know what will appeal to a home swapper reading your listing.

TICKTOCK

Swaps take time to put into effect, usually about a year but maybe longer. Most home-swap companies' directories are published once a year, with updates issued once or twice during that year. Waiting for your listing to be published and then exchanging letters and/or phone calls with prospects means that if you write today to a swap company, you probably should be planning your vacation in someone else's home 12 to 18 months from now.

VERY FEW SNAGS

The fact that swap organizations have been running for some 30 years now attests to their solidity. There are very few serious problems with this vacation style. The principal one, which does not arise often, involves traders who change their mind at the last minute, leaving the other family with no place to vacation. Another problem may arise from a difference in housekeeping standards between the two swapping families, but this problem can be avoided by each family's spelling out what it wants and expects of the other, including instructions about ordinary house cleaning, trash removal, recycling and the like.

Problems, however, are not typical with this vacation style. Swappers are sophisticated folk who, while making their own vacation plans, still manage to think about whoever will be staying in their home. They usually arrange to have a neighbor pop in occasionally, and they often leave brochures and other tourist information in the house before they leave. And they affix little Post-it® notes on appliances with operating instructions. Traders, in other words, can be very thoughtful.

What about insurance? Because swappers are pretty much guests in your home—no money changes hands—the typical homeowners or automobile insurance policy covers them. You might check your coverage with your insurance agent, though, before you leave.

FOR MORE INFORMATION

Here are two swap clubs you might contact:

Vacation Exchange Club
PO Box 650
Key West, FL 33041
800-638-3481 or 305-294-3720
The charge is $60 a year for a directory and updates.

Intervac International
PO Box 590504
San Francisco, CA 94159
800-756-HOME

A year's membership is $62 plus postage; $55 for seniors. The directory carries more than 8,000 listings in 36 countries. Intervac US is an affiliate of Intervac International, and publishes a U.S.-only directory containing some 2,000 listings. There is one annual publication. A listing costs $35. The address and phone number are the same as Intervac International's.

Home Exchange Vacationing: Your Guide to Free Accommodations by Bill and Mary Barbour, 1996, Rutledge Hill Press, $14.95.

KEEP IN MIND

➤ Living in someone's home in the community that interests you can help you see what life there is really like before you buy a vacation home.

➤ You need the right attitude to make this work—the experience is more important than the household items you left behind that may be broken.

➤ Be flexible about where you vacation. A community near your first-choice town could still offer you valuable insights into that area before you buy.

CHAPTER 5

Just a Bit of a Vacation Home: The Timeshare

Paula and Joe Fleisher certainly enjoyed one terrific vacation last year. Actually, they enjoyed three of them.

In the summer, the Fleishers, along with two couples who are close friends of theirs, spent two weeks in Scotland, a visit coinciding with the Edinburgh Festival, which they attended.

In September it was a week in the Caribbean for just the two of them, soaking up some sun. Later that year the Fleishers, who live in Connecticut, hopped up to New Hampshire for a long weekend at the foot of the White Mountains. They closed out the year by reserving a January week in Mexico.

In each of their getaways they stayed at top-flight resorts in three- and sometimes four-bedroom apartments, with views of ocean, lakes or mountains, swimming pools and tennis courts—all of the amenities of any top resort.

They brought back souvenirs from those trips, but hotel bills were not among them. The Fleishers simply traded the four-week timeshare they own in Hawaii for other lodgings around the world. Ten years ago they paid $10,000 for four weeks in a one-bedroom apartment on the big island of Hawaii, which was still somewhat underdeveloped (or beautifully underdeveloped as some might say). They have not been back there since, preferring to vacation in other spots around the world.

If you want to learn about the best use of a timeshare apartment, the Fleishers are a splendid example. Theirs is low-cost, but not no-cost, travel. There are some administrative fees attached to timesharing, but those charges are nowhere near the rate for a superior hotel room—let alone a furnished apartment—for several people for a week or two. Being able to cook some meals in an apartment kitchen is another bonus. Even just making morning coffee, and having something to eat with it, is convenient and cost saving.

"I'm ecstatic that we bought it," Paula Fleisher says of their timeshare purchase. "It not only has enabled us to travel, it has *encouraged* us to travel. You don't have that money barrier of hotel fees."

WHAT A TIMESHARE IS—AND IS NOT

Let's start with what a timeshare is not, for that is important but frequently misunderstood.

A timeshare is not a real estate investment. You are not building equity or not very likely making any money at all holding on to your purchase over the years. What you *are* doing is buying a week or two, or a month or even a season, of guaranteed vacation time in a spot for 20 or 30 years or for the life of the resort. Your purchase can be a fee simple ownership, which gives you a deed to your apartment, or a right-to-use lease, which is just that—the right to use Apartment 35 the first week in July for the length of the lease.

There are some slight management variations among resorts. One unusual practice is found at the Disney Vacation Clubs, where buyers purchase points rather than blocks of time. The points can be used at other Disney resorts or in trading apartments through timeshare swap companies.

Did You Know. . .

. . . that Florida has the most timeshare resorts in this country? The Sunshine State boasts 230 of them. California comes in second with 68, quite a drop from first place. Those statistics come from a 1993 study by the American Residential Development Association (ARDA), the Washington, D.C.–based main trade group for the industry.

Fully furnished timeshare apartments range from studios (the living room has a sofa bed) to three- or four-bedroom apartments and even cottages. (Camp sites and boats can also be sold on this principle, but here we concentrate on furnished apartments, the most common form of timeshare ownership.)

A timeshare community might be very fancy indeed, built brand-new and featuring all the "bells and whistles" of any top-flight resort. You will probably see one or two, even as many as five, swimming pools, one or two tennis courts, a golf course, boating facilities, riding and jogging trails, kiddy playgrounds, exercise rooms, restaurants, a small grocery store and many other amenities to interest and/or pamper you.

Or you can buy into a "resort" that is a building converted from another use, sometimes a hotel or motel, to a timeshare community. Usually these have no amenities at all or perhaps just a pool. Called conversions, they are, for the most part, found in oceanfront communities or other high-tourism areas where a spot with no facilities can do quite well anyway. Purchasing a conversion, of course, is not going to cost as much as a four-star resort, but it can provide many enjoyable holiday weeks and be quite affordable.

ENTER THE BIG GUNS AND RESPECTABILITY

The timeshare concept, also occasionally known as interval ownership, traveled to the United States from Switzerland in the 1960s. However, it did not get off to a solid start here, and in the 1970s had developed a reputation for fly-by-night salespeople and shady practices. Not all developers, of course, were sleazy but there were enough to cause consumer eyes to roll at the mention of the word *timeshare.* Sales stalled.

By the late 1980s, however, changes began occurring. Most states had laws regulating timeshare sales more strictly. Also in the last decade, major names in the hospitality industry, such as Marriott, Disney, Hyatt and Hilton, entered the business with deluxe resorts, solidly run. These were names America trusted. If *they* were selling timeshares, well . . .

Today, these companies continue to open new resorts and do very well indeed. Marriott, for example, has sold out its resorts in Orlando, Florida, and Hilton Head, South Carolina. Disney even has plans for a resort in New York's Times Square, albeit still a few years down the road.

All of this is *not* to say that sleazy—even illegal—tactics by some developers and high-pressure sales tactics no longer continue. In spite of changes, it is still *caveat emptor.*

A Free Lunch?

Should you take advantage of promotions you receive in the mail inviting you to a few free (or very low-cost) days in a timeshare resort? Sure, if you are seriously considering that resort, might be interested in taking a look at some timeshare communities in the same immediate area, and do not whip out your checkbook to buy before you leave.

Take questions with you to the host resort, and be sure they are answered to your satisfaction at the sales talks you will have to attend. Then go home and mull over the purchase. When you are sure, then buy.

WHERE TO FIND TIMESHARE COMMUNITIES

Timeshare resorts are all over the world. A 1995 report by the American Resort Development Association (ARDA) showed that the United States led in the number of timeshare projects with 1,546, or 37.3 percent of the worldwide total. There are 1.7 million Americans who own timeshares, both in this country and abroad. Worldwide, more than 3 million households own a timeshare unit.

Timeshares can be found in desert communities, ski areas, ocean and lakeside towns, and rural locales that may be 40 or 50 miles away from much of anything.

Timeshares are not typically found in big cities. Keep that in mind if you are a city person and not interested in tennis, golf, and similar activities, but prefer instead museums, theater and shopping.

Little by little, timeshares *have* been moving into urban areas. They are in San Francisco and New Orleans, for example, and plans are under way for more in other cities. If you opt for an urban address, keep in mind that timeshare buildings in land-scarce cities are not likely to have the amenities you'll find in resorts. Many of them will be conversions from existing buildings, too, which is neither good nor bad. The scarcity of city timeshares, incidentally, applies abroad as well as to American resort properties.

Another point to remember here: Because most timeshare resorts are well out of city limits, you will probably have to rent a car if you are flying to your destination. And speaking of driving, another benefit of timesharing is that it lets you vacation as far away, or as close, as you would like when family and priorities change. There is always a resort to visit.

Cathy and Bill Rogers live in northern Florida and own two time-share weeks in Hilton Head and one in Orlando. They have enjoyed us-ing them all, especially the Orlando week when their children were small. But now it's different. "We have kids in college," Bill explains, "and until they get through we won't be doing too much flying. We've toured the Southeast rather extensively, though, sometimes bringing friends with us to a resort as the apartments are spacious." Coming up for the couple: a week in Williamsburg, Virginia.

Bill Rogers has become very much involved in timeshare ownership. A few years ago he started a timeshare users group on the Internet. There's more about that organization under "For More Information."

TIME: WHAT MATTERS MOST IN A TIMESHARE PURCHASE

When you are ready to begin timeshare shopping, study time—the week(s) you choose at the resort that interests you. Most complexes have a high season, a serious off-season and some time of neither, all based on the activities in that particular resort area.

The value of your timeshare apartment lies not in what the devel-oper is touting as exceptional furnishings. Its value is, first, the week you have purchased; second, the geographic location of your complex; and, third, the facilities at that resort.

The times to buy that are most in demand for trades are summer, the week between Christmas and New Year's, and the long President's Day weekend in February. In ski areas, other midwinter weeks are also in high demand.

Let's look at some examples of how this works. Time in Hawaii is considered prime year-round—everyone wants to visit any time of the year. Prime time at Florida timeshares is also January 1 through December 31, and the same is true for much or all of the Caribbean and Bermuda.

If you buy into a complex in, say, New Hampshire, though, you will find the in-season probably runs from mid-June through mid-October, covering summer and then closing after fall's foliage days. It picks up again a few days before Christmas and continues to early April when skiers crowd the resorts. The "shoulder" weeks, the "not-quite-in-and-not-quite-off" season, run from mid-May to mid-June and then from mid-October to the end of October, when the weather is still quite pleasant. The off-season in New Hampshire is likely to be from early April to the middle of May and from the first of November to around December 20. Those days are low-season because it is usually too warm for snow and far too cold for warm-weather activities.

All of this information is important because you can trade based on what you have to offer. The Fleishers travel around the world—in season—because their four weeks in Hawaii are prime swap material. If you buy a week in New Hampshire in the off-season, you do not have the same bargaining chip. You will find it difficult, some say impossible, to swap, and certainly for top-of-the-line resorts in season. That is not to say, of course, that you can't enjoy vacations there each year if that is what you prefer.

Remember the information above when a developer tells you that you can trade your week and travel the world. It depends on *which* week you buy.

Incidentally, you should remember that you can pass on your timeshare unit to your heirs.

POINTS TO CONSIDER BEFORE BUYING

Does a timeshare sound pretty good to you, and are you eager to buy? Here are some points to think and talk about during the decision-making process:

- Be sure you will make good use of your timeshare unit through regular vacations there. Perhaps you will want to offer some time to family members. Many owners give a week's vacation to an adult child as a graduation or other gift. The Fleishers are giving their daughter and future son-in-law a week in Wales for their upcoming honeymoon. Because this is not an investment, it is pointless to buy a timeshare just to hold it.
- Timeshare costs range from around $10,000 per week to over $15,000 for the newest, spiffiest apartments at luxury resorts.

Becoming Hot, Even in the Cold

Branson, Missouri, is rising fast in popularity as a sizable timeshare resort area. This small town has become a mecca for country music singers and other entertainers who not only perform but have also built their own theaters there. The area also boasts other tourist draws. Branson used to be lively only during the summer, but vacationers are crowding theaters now all year (although timeshare resorts are still likely to have specific high- and low-season weeks).

Speaking of timesharing and its new respectable image, how does the name Lawrence Welk sound? Pretty legitimate? The Welk Resort Center, owned by the late entertainer's son, is one of the growing number of timeshare resorts (this one with a 2,300-seat theater) springing up in Branson.

Think about how you will pay for that purchase. Long-term financing from the developer might be possible. Lending institutions are not eager to offer mortgages on timeshares because most resorts are probably far from the lenders and the value of your unit, and whether it is well or poorly maintained, depends a good deal on outside forces, such as the developer, maintenance programs and even competition in the area. If you are buying a resale unit (more about them later), you might be able to take over the seller's financing. Timeshare purchases that are leased-time, rather than fee simple, are usually financed with a personal loan.

- Think about related fees. When we talked about the Fleishers' great vacations, we said there *are* administrative costs to timeshare owning. Besides the price of your apartment, you have to pay an annual maintenance fee that usually runs $300 to $600 or so for each week. This fee usually goes up periodically, so be sure you can afford higher maintenance fees over the years.
- Trading provides a much lower charge that we discuss shortly. Moneywise, you'll get the best use from a timeshare if you take a few people with you on vacation so that the savings on hotel rooms (and perhaps restaurant meals) become quite pronounced.

- There is another cost to consider. While you will be cutting out hotel bills, there is still airfare to your destination if you cannot drive there and perhaps a car rental as well.

QUESTIONS TO ASK AT THE COMMUNITY YOU ARE CONSIDERING

The most important ingredient of a successful resort (aside from its location) is its management. Check out the developer with your state attorney general's office and local department of consumer affairs to see if any complaints have been filed before you have a serious talk about buying at that resort's sales office.

Questions to ask at the sales office:

- What kind of title will I receive?
- Am I getting fee simple ownership or a long-term lease? For how many years?
- How will you help me pay? (Be sure you understand all the terms of financing.)
- Who runs the owners association or other governing body? Does everyone vote? Or is it the developer who manages the property?
- How much is my annual maintenance fee? How has that risen over the last three or four years? What part of that fee is tax deductible? (Your share of property taxes might come to somewhere around $30 a year for your week.)
- What other expenses will I have? Any special fees for cleaning, using the pool and other amenities?
- What about the budget for this resort? Is it adequate for the size of the development? Is there a reserve fund for emergency expenses? (Ask to see something in writing.)
- May I have the names of some other owners here? (The developer should not mind giving you a list of some who have bought there for you to contact.)
- Do you have access to an exchange network so that I can trade my apartment? (Keep in mind those foregoing cautions about good weeks for trading.)
- Are there are any benefits to me if I don't use my week (for example, sharing in any rental fee a developer might secure)?
- Will you try to find a buyer for my unit if I choose to sell? What are the conditions? (Some of the larger developers, such as Marriott,

do offer sales programs for their owners. Resorts that try to sell owners' units will add charges for their services, reflected in the price you finally realize for your apartment.)

On Second Thought . . .

Most states offer a cooling-off period to allow timeshare buyers to change their minds about a purchase, even if they have signed a contract to buy. Be sure to check the state where you are buying. That time can be 3 days or maybe as many as 15. Call that state's attorney general's office.

THE BEST BUY

You will probably want to visit new complexes and see just how posh some resorts are and what amenities they offer buyers for the price. When it's time to act, though, the best deal is likely to be found in buying directly from a seller. Buying a "used" timeshare is not a bad thing.

"It's really a resale when you get there anyhow," notes Bill Rogers. Adding that if you buy your timeshare in July, and it's for one week the following June, he says, "There will probably be about 50 families who will have stayed there ahead of you." In well-established resorts, apartments are always maintained to look good for new arrivals as are lobbies and other common areas.

You can save a lot of money buying a used apartment. How to find sellers? They advertise in newspapers, both local and national, and on the Internet. And, as mentioned, some resorts will have resales in their sales office.

Remember time and location in buying from a seller. A $3,500 timeshare for an off-week in a not very well known location can be a terrific deal for you if it is a well-managed resort and you plan to spend that week each year enjoying yourself there. If you want to trade, though, your "steal" is no bargain.

THE DELIGHTS OF TRADING

If the appeal of a timeshare is using your week for around-the-country or around-the-world travel, you will, soon after your purchase, find yourself in the wonderful world of timeshare trading.

Try It Before You Buy It

It would be wise to take a one-week vacation, or even a long weekend, at a timeshare resort before plunking down money to buy. Most resorts rent apartments not being used by their owners for a wide range of rates, from perhaps $40 a day to $100. While you are enjoying your holiday, ask management and fellow vacationers plenty of questions about the complex.

Some large developers with several timeshare resorts—Fairfield Communities, the Arkansas-based developer, is one of them—have a swap program within their own company for owners who want to trade their week for one at another Fairfield resort. Among specific timeshare trade companies, the largest is Resort Condominiums International, based in Indianapolis, Indiana. You can call them at 800-724-7744. Interval International, headquartered in Miami, Florida, also arranges swaps and has a considerable number of listings. They are at 305-666-1861.

You should expect to spend under $100 for an annual membership fee with a trading firm and around $100 to exchange a unit.

A FEW WORDS ABOUT SELLING

It can sometimes be hard to sell a timeshare apartment. Newer, fancier resorts are always opening, attracting the buyers you want if you own desirable time in an attractive community. If you don't, however, then you're likely to have a particularly rough time.

Some of the tonier resorts will, as we have mentioned, handle the resale of your week (but remember, if there are any units still unsold in that resort, they'll try to sell them first). You might have some loss from your purchase price because of the fees you must pay the resale office. How can you buy and profit? If you have purchased into a top-flight resort in prime timeshare weeks, your week *might* appreciate over the years.

Late in 1995 the director of resales for Marriott told the *New York Times* that owners in the 20 or so Marriott timeshare resorts "can probably expect to get 70 percent to 110 percent of what they paid for [their units]." Overall, on average, sellers recoup 50 to 75 percent of their purchase price.

The Fleishers stand to make *some* money if they ever decide to sell their four weeks in Hawaii. Their paying $2,500 per week was extremely reasonable. Also, over the last ten years the coastal areas of the island of Hawaii have become busier with development—new stores, restaurants, apartment buildings—and will probably appeal to more buyers.

How can you sell a timeshare unit if you are left on your own? You might advertise in your daily newspaper and perhaps in national publications, such as *USA Today*. Advertise on bulletin boards around town, in your college alumni newsletter, on the Internet and just about any other place that occurs to you. You might ask your developer to recommend a broker where your timeshare is located who knows that special market. This will cost you a percentage of the sale—maybe 25 percent or more. You might have to pay several hundred dollars up front. Be very careful here as this area is rife with swindles. Never sign with a broker who will guarantee selling your timeshare. No one can assure that. It's best to check out all individuals or companies with your local consumer affairs office.

You might find, though, that with the opportunity to trade your apartment for travel all around the world, you will *never* want to sell your timeshare!

FOR MORE INFORMATION

For tips on buying a timeshare and other consumer information on the subject, contact:

American Resort Development Association
1220 L Street NW
Washington, DC 20005
202-371-6700

Resort Property Owners Association
PO Box 2395
Northbrook, IL 60062
847-291-0710

Internet users can join Timeshare Users Group (TUG), an organization that was formed by Bill Rogers. This is a noncommercial association of timeshare owners offering advice, ranking resorts and running classified advertisements to buy or sell apartments. The membership fee is $15 a year. Its information is on computer, so log in and see exactly what TUG has to offer. The address is http:\\www.timeshare-users-group.com.

K E E P   I N   M I N D

➤ A timeshare is not a real estate investment but rather the purchase of a specific week or two (or more) in a furnished apartment at a particular resort for a specified number of years.

➤ It's the time of year you buy, and the resort you select, not the fancy furnishings of that complex, that determine your ability to make great trades.

➤ Selling when you want can be a problem. Don't expect a profit.

CHAPTER 6

On the Road Again: The RV as Vacation Home

Ah, the open road. Not for you, you say, the confines of a vacation house or apartment. *Your* second home will be on wheels, and you will drive from one fascinating locale to another.

You certainly can do just that with a recreational vehicle—an RV. You can visit tourist sites or stop by and see the kids for a week or two. Or those former neighbors you were so close to who now live 400 miles away. With your RV you can enjoy ever-changing landscapes without paying expensive hotel bills or, with some vehicles, any restaurant tabs either.

There is another advantage to the RV lifestyle: the camaraderie that exists among owners. You will make new friends at the various campgrounds where you stay a night or more. Many facilities have lively social programs of potluck suppers, dances and bingo. And through camping clubs you can all meet at conventions and rallies.

THERE ARE RVs AND THERE ARE RVs

You will have a dazzling variety of vehicles from which to choose when you decide to buy a recreational vehicle. There are mini-motorhomes, bilevels, fold-down camping trailers and on and on. You can have as simple or as fancy a vehicle as you like—or can afford. Some have all the necessities for year-round living, including state-of-the-art kitchens, while others offer simply a place to bed down.

You can pay anywhere from five figures for a used, simple RV to more than $300,000 for a model that will make your eyes pop. An average price, however, is $40,000 to $55,000. RVs are purchased like cars, and like cars most of them depreciate in value over time, although not at the same speed as autos. That's *most* of them. Some vintage vehicles—for instance, some of the round-domed, silver Airstream trailers dating to the 1950s—actually bring prices now higher than their original value. Antique RVs can, like antique cars, be quite valuable.

WHERE TO GO

If it is allowed in a residential neighborhood you are visiting, you can park your RV in that home's driveway. Or you can stop at one of the nation's 16,000 rental campgrounds. Rentals run from about $7 a night in national parks for just the space and no hookups to $40–$50 for top-of-the-line campgrounds in a prime location in season with hookups for utilities and lively entertainment programs. If you rent for the long term—the entire winter, say—your charges will be lower.

Uh-Oh

Some campgrounds do not allow pets. Some, for retirees, do not permit children, although those could be long-term facilities and not for vacationers just passing through. Still, if you'll be taking kids or Fido with you, better ask about regulations when making reservations.

PREPARING TO HIT THE ROAD

There are a few points—and pretty major ones some of them are, too—to think about before you head for the interstate in your new (to you, anyway) RV.

RVs are *big*. You'll want to practice driving these unfamiliar vehicles before taking to the open road. Many owners haul their car behind the vehicle when they vacation so they can use it for short jaunts to restaurants or stores when parked in a campground. Driving an RV with a car behind it is a *lot* of maneuvering and will take some practice.

Work the numbers here, too. Yes, RVing can afford you a relatively inexpensive holiday, but it does cost money, even when you're not on the road. Besides campground fees, and perhaps restaurant meals if your motor home has no cooking facilities (and even if it does you might want some meals out), you'll have to factor in gasoline. That can be expensive, and you are likely to get just eight or so miles per gallon, maybe less.

Here is one owner's experience with mileage: Tom Muller and his wife, Carlene, live full-time in Maine, and for several years have spent vacations from work traveling in their Winnebago. They have journeyed from Florida to Alaska, from the Maritimes to Montana.

When the Mullers drove to Alaska in 1993, Muller saw that two-thirds of their trip was consumed just getting there and back. Those were long traveling days with little time to enjoy the wonders of that northernmost state once they arrived. Retired RVers have the time for all that traveling, but Muller is still working and so began thinking of a better way to combine RVing with sightseeing, fitting them both into a typical one- to three-week vacation.

So Muller began The RV Exchange on the Internet, which matched RV owners across the country who wanted to swap their home on wheels for someone else's. The exchange is now defunct, but the principle is a good one. Let's say you have an RV in Washington State and you want to tour New England. Instead of driving east, you fly to your destination, pick up your trader's RV and then begin tooling around New England. That RV owner is doing the same with your RV back in Washington. Neither of you charges the other for use of the vehicle.

Swapping saves time (more days of actual vacationing at the area you choose), energy (less unnecessary driving) and probably money, too, even when you include airfares (unless you have a family of five). At seven or eight miles per gallon of gasoline, you'll cover a lot of miles by RV from one coast to the other. You might find an RV owner by advertising in a magazine or newspaper or on the Internet.

"If you're trying to stretch the life of a single RV purchase over 20, even 30, years," Muller explains, "knocking the mileage down from 10,000 per trip to 3,000 is very attractive." Muller says that many buyers do indeed intend to own only one RV, and when it "dies," that's it.

Muller adds that it's best to trade with fellow owners because renting one's RV to someone who does not own, and is not familiar with, one of those behemoths can be particularly wearing on the vehicle, resulting in high bills for repairs. "Somebody who has a very sophisticated powerboat or sailboat might be acceptable," Muller says, "because so many of the systems are the same. But we used to get calls from people who wanted to swap their condo for an RV and that we didn't do."

The Family That Vacations Together . . .

Janet Groene, coauthor of *Living Aboard Your RV* (see "For More Information"), suggests that when you rent a home on wheels to get a taste of life on the road before you buy, you should vacation only with the person or persons you will be traveling with regularly. After three or four weeks you will learn whether you can survive coping with laundry, rainy days stuck inside, cooking and other aspects of traveling that are not always fun and games. Not to mention just being with each other 24 hours a day!

THEN THERE'S . . .

Paperwork. You will have to pay to register your vehicle and insure it. Maintenance costs should be added to your calculations of expenses too. One way to learn about all of these likely cash outlays is by talking to those who sell RVs. "Find a dealer and pick his brain," says Tom Muller. "That's what they're there for and most of them do a pretty good job." You can also join one or more of the groups listed under "For More Information," taking advantage of any printed material they offer and talking with fellow members about their experiences.

Another important consideration: Where will you park your vehicle when you are at home? Communities that have an owners association—and they can be single-family home neighborhoods as well as condominiums—are likely to prohibit an RV in the driveway for more than a handful of days once or twice a year. If you can't leave it with a family member, you will have to pay for storage. Will that mean a very large self-storage unit, or do you have other options?

MORE MONEY TALK

Many RV buyers pay cash for their vehicles. Financing is treated much like a car loan, probably with an interest rate two to four percentage points above the prime rate or a little higher than the typical automobile loan. The Internal Revenue Service considers recreational vehicles second homes under certain conditions. There's more about that in Chapter 19.

RENTING FIRST

Before embarking on this major buying adventure, it would be wise to rent an RV for a vacation to see how it fits "all" of you. Here, too, you will have a number of styles from which to choose. You can rent one that sleeps four and has a kitchenette and a bathroom for around $500 to $1400 a week, lower or higher depending on the season you elect. Going smaller to a vehicle that will provide only sleeping accommodations, you might spend $200 to $400.

To learn more about renting an RV, you can contact the Recreation Vehicle Rental Association, 3930 University Drive, Fairfax, Virginia 22030, or call 800-336-0355. It publishes *Who's Who, RV Rentals* for $5 and *Rental Ventures*, a book of tips for travelers. That book sells for $3, or $2.50 if you purchase the $5 publication too. You can also call Cruise America, one of the largest RV rental dealers in the country, in Miami, Florida, at 800-327-7778.

FOR MORE INFORMATION

The American Resort Development Association (ARDA) offers consumer information about buying an RV. Contact them at:

1220 L Street NW, Suite 510
Washington, DC 20005
202-371-6700

Woodall's has been covering RV news for many years and will send you a free copy of its annual *Woodall's Discover RVing*. Contact:

Woodall's Discover RVing
PO Box 5000
Lake Forest, IL 60045
800-362-7989

Living Aboard Your RV by Janet and Gordon Groene, $15.95, and *Cooking Aboard Your RV* by Janet Groene, $14.95, are both published by Ragged Mountain Press. They are available at bookstores, or you can call 800-822-8158.

For a complete list of RV clubs—there are about a dozen around the country, many offering special member discounts that reduce fees at campgrounds—contact

Recreation Vehicle Industry Association
PO Box 2999
Reston, VA 22090
703-620-6003

KEEP IN MIND

➤ Rent an RV before buying, calculate ownership costs and determine where you will park your vehicle when you are back at your primary residence.

➤ Loans for RVs are much like automobile financing.

➤ Whether you have rented or purchased your vehicle, always ask about discounts in campgrounds, RV clubs, and related services and products.

➤ There are tax allowances for this type of second home under IRS guidelines.

CHAPTER 7

Hitting the High Seas on Your Boat (They're Vacation "Homes" Too)

Perhaps your ideal second home is by the water. No, make that *on* the water. You vote for a boat!

You might have rented a boat for holidays several times in the past and now are about to take the plunge and buy one as a second home. Or you might be reading this without any previous knowledge of boating, aside from being a guest on one now and again. Boating is an absorbing pastime, with certainly far more to learn than can be offered in these few pages. We can, however, whet your appetite for more information and put you in touch with some publications and associations that will open up this world for you.

Anne M. Johnson, a writer and boating enthusiast, points out the attractions of a home on the water: "The best part of having a boat as a second home is that you can dock it anywhere you want. If you like, you can move the boat from place to place so that the trip itself becomes part of the vacation.

"You always have a waterfront home, too. If you want to see the sun rise, you take your boat to the East Coast. If you want to see it set, head for the West Coast. You can pick your view, which you certainly can't do with a house."

Anne and her husband, John, reside in the Southeast and have lived full time on their sailboat while cruising the Caribbean and local waters, and sometimes just staying home at the marina in their town. They have also, in the last several years, lived in an apartment, with the boat docked on a waterway just outside their balcony, using it just for vacations. Now they are in another apartment, and *Forever Amber II* is docked at a marina about 40 miles downriver. These days they escape to that small community for weekends and vacations, picking up the boat and leisurely sailing some inland waterways. Great lifestyle—and flexible too.

WHAT KIND OF CRAFT?

If you expect to spend 24 hours a day on your boat many days of the year, perhaps at a marina, you might consider a houseboat, which offers space and is more stable than some other craft.

Planning to navigate the high seas? The choice is yours. For cruising around the world, sailboats are noted for their economy and seaworthiness. A powerboat will serve you well, traveling the thousands of miles of inland waterways throughout this country. With a sailboat you will need more skill and attention to it than you will with turning on the engine of a powerboat. The Johnsons, for example, work on their boat at sea.

Try for a craft at least 30 to 40 feet long and 10 to 12 feet wide if you are going to live aboard comfortably for any length of time. "Comfortably" is open to interpretation, of course. You may see advertisements for boats that tout "sleeps 11." Janet Groene, a boating (and RV) writer based in Florida, says uh-huh.

"Buyers should look for a boat to *accommodate* their family and not just sleep the family," she points out. "You can get a boat that sleeps 12 people, but has only one "john" and seats only four at the table. Houseboats, though, are finally beginning to realize that people need more than one bathroom."

Showering at the marina will cut back on that line in front of the "head," but of course it will form again when you are out on the water. Groene also notes you will need adequate food storage aboard, a point to keep in mind as you look at boats.

ALL THOSE WATERWAYS

There is more to boating in this country than enjoying that sport on both coasts. America has hundreds of waterways between the two

---

Timeshares? You Bet

The timeshare concept applies to boats as well as apartments on land. You can purchase a specific block of time to spend on a particular watercraft for a designated period of time each year for as many years as your contract allows. If you'd like to learn more, you can call and talk with Robert Perkins, president of Houseboat Owners of America. See "For More Information" at the end of this chapter.

---

oceans that can be explored, providing thousands of miles of boating enjoyment to the enthusiast.

Douglas Blom, publisher of *Heartland Boating* magazine, and his wife, Molly, editor of the publication, have spent 20-plus years vacationing on their houseboat and touring heartland waterways. Doug Blom explained that a friend of his recently returned from a one-year sojourn traveling, for the most part, inland, starting from Nashville and heading south, eventually reaching Key West. Then north to New York and into Canada for a bit, and back to Tennessee. The year cost about $50,000 for boat and all on-land expenses.

Blom noted the sailor and his wife flew in their college kids periodically to join them on the boat. They ate occasionally at some spiffy dining spots, too. "They did it up right," he said. If you dream of such an odyssey, you can spend far less. Still, boating is not an inexpensive "sport," as you will learn next.

CH-CHING, CH-CHING: COST

Let's see exactly what you can expect to spend to take to the sea.

The craft itself can cost you anywhere from $20,000 for a secondhand purchase to over $1 million, a range similar to homebuying. Remember that we are talking here about boats, not floating homes, which are houses built on a barge. A barge does not move from its dock.

Slip-rental charges cut a wide swath. You can pay anywhere from $50 to $1,000 a month or more for your boat. The higher end, of course, is for a five-star marina, usually in a resort locale in high season. High season may be exactly the time you plan to take your boating vacations, so keep in mind almost everything is likely to cost you more then.

Then there are fuel costs, repairs, annual registration (every state requires a boat to be registered at fees that vary) and insurance. Insurance varies, too, according to the age of the craft, its type and size, where it is used and a number of other variables. Premiums are usually $200 to $2,000 a year.

How to pay for a dream craft, or at least the closest you can come to one right now? You can hand over cash, and a lot of buyers do. If you want a boat larger than 30 feet, you can seek what is known as a *ship's mortgage*. That is similar to a house mortgage even though your boat is not real estate.

You can apply at almost any bank, and some credit unions, for a loan. The down payment requirement is likely to be 10 to 25 percent. Some banks will waive that, but you might want to put something down anyway. There could be negative amortization with your craft somewhere along the line. That means the boat may depreciate in value faster than you can pay it off, which you will want to avoid.

Most boats, like cars, do depreciate. But like recreational vehicles, which we discussed in the previous chapter, they do so at a slower rate than automobiles. There are always exceptions, of course. Some boats hold their value to the time of resale, bringing the sellers almost what was paid for the craft or, in a few instances, more.

Back to your mortgage: The length of the loan is likely to be a minimum of 12 years and a maximum of 20. You might be wise to ask for 15 years to avoid the possibility of negative amortization with the longer term.

Interest rates usually are lower than with an auto loan and not a whole lot higher than for a real estate purchase. You also might want to look into a home equity loan on your present residence to finance the boat.

Finally, you will certainly be interested to know that the federal government allows an income deduction for your boat in certain circumstances. See Chapter 19.

RENT FIRST

A frequent tip to rent first offered throughout this book is especially important with boating. Before purchasing a boat, try some boating vacations as a renter. You might be able to locate a rental near your home, or you could elect to fly to a vacation spot and rent there.

If you have some experience at the helm you can be the captain, or you can rent a boat with a captain included in the rental fee. Of course, when you eventually buy, you might rent out your boat if you choose (only to experienced sailors, owners say, if you want to preserve the craft).

Where can you find rentals? Anne Johnson points out that every state has at least one place that rents boats. Check your Yellow Pages under "Boats" or "Charters."

FOR MORE INFORMATION

Robert Perkins, president of the Houseboat Association of America, can answer questions about buying and using a houseboat, planning travel routes, and any other houseboat-related queries from a member or nonmember of the association, including questions about boat time-shares.

Membership in the association costs $15 a year, which brings a bi-monthly newsletter and the ability to be put in touch by the member-ship office with a person or family who has made a trip or a purchase you're planning or who can otherwise be of some assistance. Contact:

Houseboat Association of America
2940 North Rhett Ave.
Charleston, SC 29405
803-744-6581

Heartland Boating Magazine
PO Box 1067
Martin, TN 38237

The subscription rate for one year (seven issues) is $16.95. You can, however, enter a subscription but if you do not want to continue re-ceiving the magazine after receiving your first copy, you can mark "cancel" on the invoice.

You can also check out the magazine on the World Wide Web at www.gsn.com.

Sailing on a Budget by Anne M. Johnson (Betterway Books).

Florida Under Sail by Janet and Gordon Groene (Country Roads Press, $9.95). At bookstores, or you can call 800-642-6420.

KEEP IN MIND

➤ It's a big country with not only two oceans but also thousands of miles of inland waterways to explore.

➤ Rent a boat for a few vacations before buying.

➤ When you do buy, key your purchase to the types of waterways you will be navigating.

CHAPTER 8

Buying Land and Building a Home

For some any home is a vacation home. For others, the dream is a second home that is newly constructed just for them. It is the locale *they* choose, the land *they* purchase, the home *they* design or at least have specially built.

Is that you? Is the individualist in you singing a few bars of "My Way" about now?

The great thing about land, as the saying goes, is that it has to be valuable because they aren't making any more of it. Land in vacation areas, in particular, is a potential gold mine, we all believe. They are certainly not making any more oceans or mountains. Manmade lakes can still crop up, but eventually the end will be in sight there, too, in and around desirable vacation settings.

THE GOOD EARTH

If you have flown any distance across America, you have seen from your plane window just how much vacant land there is in this country: miles and miles and miles of it.

Miles and miles and miles of it, however, is totally uninhabitable. As you will see when you look for land to buy, there is "good" land and there is acreage neither you nor anyone else will want to buy. Here's how to choose just the right spot:

> "It is a comfortable feeling to know that you stand on your own ground. Land is about the only thing that can't fly away."
>
> Anthony Trollope (1815–1882)

- Buy land now only if you plan to build a home on that site fairly soon. Land is an illiquid investment—it is difficult to sell if you need cash in a hurry, tougher than selling a home. Also, if you plan to hold a lot a number of years before building—maybe you plan to build a retirement place eventually—many things can arise to keep you from realizing your dream home there, as we'll discuss.
- The environment is a hot-hot-hot issue these days when purchasing land. Much land in vacation areas is now protected, not only from overbuilding, but from any building at all. Look at environmental decisions in the state and community that interests you. See what government agencies are planning to buy for "land bank" or other purposes and where they'll be putting a moratorium on building. You might find you can't buy a lot where you would like because much, if not all, of the vacant land there is protected from development. Or, worse, if you have bought a lot, you may be prohibited from building on it when you are ready.

  Not all curbs on growth come from politicians' decisions. Many residents of vacation communities have been organizing to fight additional growth in their towns because, they say, resources (roads, schools, etc.) are rapidly becoming strained. Those folks are putting pressure on their politicians to hold the population down.
- Since vacation communities are particularly desirable, you'll want to know what the master plan for the town you like has to say about building—especially building new roads and widening existing thoroughfares. You wouldn't want to buy acreage the government will soon seize for road construction. Or you wouldn't want to see a strip mall constructed behind your quiet little patch of paradise three years after you have moved in. Be

sure to know how your area is zoned and what could be built next to you a few years down the road as the area continues to boom.

- Also check utilities. Is the lot you want serviced by public sewer and water? If not, you will need a septic system and a well.

A Raw Deal?

"Raw land" is acreage available for building but lacking utilities or such improvements as water, electricity and roads. "Improved land," on the other hand, has these essentials for development.

- Can the land be used as a homesite? Is the lot large enough, following local zoning laws, for construction of a home?

  This is an important point. In your haste to buy what seems like perfect land in or near a vacation setting, you must first be certain you can build when you decide the time is right. How frustrating, alarming—horrible!—it would be to find that you cannot erect a home because your lot is too small, not just for the house you want but for *any* home.
- You will want to have the soil checked. You might have to add topsoil or take some away from your lot. A high-water table, or a ground not stable enough to support a house, could run into quite an expense. Be especially wary of acreage over a landfill, where flooding can occur frequently as that water table rises.
- Another important point: Manufactured homes are very popular these days (these are houses assembled in a factory with the parts shipped to the owner's lot, where they are assembled to become a house). You could be planning one for your lot, but you should know there are some municipalities with regulations against them. Be sure they are allowed where you want to buy.
- Be certain you will get clear title to the land.

THE NEW-HOME DEVELOPMENT

You see "Whispering Pines" and love the look of that new community. Eventually there will be 65 single-family homes there, plus a pool and tennis courts. Right now, though, there are just three model homes, a sales office, and what looks like two homes under construction. Should you buy a lot there?

You could get an excellent price for land, especially if it is farther back in the development, away from the main entrance. The developer might also finance it for you, which is not that common with a land purchase. If the development is a success, prices for lots and homes will rise, and there you will be with your earlier, lower-priced land.

The other side of the coin is that the development is not a success or the developer goes bust, and construction does not continue as far back as your lot. Maybe the pool and tennis courts never do make it past the drawing-board stage. You are sort of all by yourself back there.

You can avoid that scenario by checking out the developer before signing a sales contract. Is the developer familiar with that geographic area? What else has he or she built there? Are there any complaints by homebuyers or landholders against the developer on record with the area's department of consumer affairs or the state's attorney general's office?

TALKING MONEY

Your lot could cost $500 or $250,000, depending, of course, on that magic word: location. Generally speaking, you will find that the more road frontage there is on an already completed thoroughfare, the more valuable a piece of land there will be. The more expense required to develop the land, the cheaper your purchase price (but don't forget to consider the money you'll have to spend clearing the land, bringing in utilities and maybe even creating a new or better access road).

How much to offer for the land that interests you? You can bargain here the way you do with the asking price for a house. For a large lot you might want to hire an appraiser. If an appraisal comes in substantially below the seller's asking price, the appraisal could help you convince the seller your offer is a reasonable one. Don't forget, before you begin negotiating, to factor in the taxes you will have to pay on your lot, insurance, and interest on any loan.

Be sure you don't make an offer until you are certain the land has met the earlier-mentioned qualifications: there are no environmental restrictions to building, the lot is large enough for a house, and the like.

Generally, vacant land is a cash purchase, or the seller offers the buyer a loan. Some banks are now making loans for land if the buyer can show proof that he or she has a builder and is ready to start with the construction of a home on that site. You might also want to contact mortgage brokers, who will know lenders who make these kinds of loans.

Since we are talking about a vacation home here, a good deal of your success in negotiating price, and a loan from the seller if that is what you want, will depend on how motivated that individual is. That's true in any realty transaction, of course, but if you are bidding for particularly desirable recreational land, you might find few seller concessions.

A Familiar Refrain

As we have been pointing out, you must pay special attention to the resale value of whatever real estate you purchase—both vacant land and the home you build on that land. Choose what is likely to appeal to other buyers so that you'll have no trouble selling when you want to move.

BUILDING A HOME ON YOUR LAND

Once you have the land, you will probably want your vacation home as soon as possible.

You have several choices. You might be interested in an architect-designed house, the one you have been mulling over in your mind for several years. If that's your choice, give some thought to engaging an architect in or near that community, whether it is 60 miles or 600 miles or more from your permanent residence. A local will know about soil conditions, how the weather affects siding and many other details that could escape someone not familiar with the climate, and indeed day-to-day living, in that community.

Another option is a manufactured home. We have already discussed the importance of being able to erect one on your lot if you choose, so the legality of these homes in your community is not likely to be a concern at this stage. Manufactured homes have become extremely popular over the last decade or so, and in fact there were more than 300,000 of them sold in 1995, many for second-home purposes.

Manufactured homes come in a variety of styles, from quite posh to very simple. An average three-bedroom, two-bath house, loaded with such amenities as a fireplace, will cost around $45,000, including installation. You can also spend as much as $100,000 plus. Carports and garages are extra, as are landscaping costs.

The Manufactured Housing Institute (MHI) can send you all kinds of printed material about these dwellings. They can also put you in touch with the MHI office in your state. Contact:

Manufactured Housing Institute
2101 Wilson Blvd., Suite 610
Arlington, VA 22201
703-558-0400

The government can help with your purchase, too. They offer *How To Buy a Manufactured Home* for 50 cents from the Consumer Information Center, Dept. 429W, Pueblo, CO 81009.

Would you like to see a log cabin go up on your land? For information about those manufactured homes contact:

Building Systems Council
National Association of Home Builders
15th & M Streets NW
Washington, DC 20005
202-822-0576

KEEP IN MIND

➤ Not all land is valuable. Do enough homework to be able to separate the wheat from the chaff, so to speak.

➤ Don't buy a lot that is not part of a new-home development too many years before you build there. Too many things can change around your lot—and not always for the better.

➤ Make certain you *can* build on the lot that interests you, especially if you are interested in a manufactured home.

CHAPTER 9

A Broad Look at Buying Abroad

You want sand . . . but on Caribbean shores or you want great skiing . . . but farther afield than American resorts. Or perhaps you'd like a small castle or condominium or chalet out in the country—but in someone else's country. You just want to go international with your vacation home.

There is a lot to be said for having a place outside U.S. borders. If a second home is supposed to be a change from routine, having that spot on foreign soil is truly getting away from it all. You'll learn about another country, perhaps an entire geographical area, while you're holidaying. You might pick up another language. And let's face it, hordes of friends and relatives are not likely to drop in when you're out of the country. (Or are they? See the *Just Say "No"* box in this chapter.)

WHERE THE BUYS ARE

Some parts of the Caribbean, as you might expect, are popular with second-home buyers. Mexico is hot these days in more ways than one. Because of that country's economic ups and downs, the dollar value there is good right now. The American dollar is also worth about one-third more than the Canadian dollar, making a second home in Canada an excellent dollar-for-dollar value. The appeal of our neighbor to the north is different from that of Latin America and the islands. Canada is a sporty, outdoor-oriented country popular with people who love to fish, hunt, ski and hike. From the days when Franklin Roosevelt and his family summered at Campobello Island off the coast of New Brunswick to modern times when ski villages being marketed by a Vancouver-based developer called IntraWest seem to achieve rapid success, Canada has maintained its popularity.

Jane Lears, editorial director of *International Living,* a monthly newsletter for those living overseas or planning to, or those whose work takes them abroad, agrees that Mexico, including Baja California, is enjoying quite a bit of attention from Americans these days, particularly from those looking for a retirement home.

"Honduras is another choice," Lears adds, "and Belize." She notes both have good prices to offer homebuyers and a low cost of living. "Costa Rica, too," she continues, "although less now than it used to be. Ireland is also very popular and inexpensive." And, Lear concludes, Great Britain draws many Americans.

Perhaps none of these countries quite hits the spot for you (you're not even sure where Belize is). Then, no doubt, you can easily find your bliss somewhere else. Remember Peter Mayle and his best-selling books from Provence? As you know, he headed to that part of southern France from his primary residence in England to seek a vacation home. He became so enraptured with the area he wrote *A Year in Provence,* followed by several other books, some of them also set in and around his home there. Now that region, probably in part because of Mayle's writings, is more popular than ever for second-home buyers and vacationers. Surely there is a country whose siren call you hear as Mayle did France's?

Your choice might be Portugal, where you've vacationed for a number of years. Or Italy, where you still have relatives, or a Caribbean island you can reach in a hurry when February seems endless in your Ohio town. Or you may want to mingle with Europeans who frequent the French Riviera, the Spanish coast, Greece or Turkey for their annual vacation escapes and where they've invested in property. Israel has experienced scary times, but such Mediterranean resorts as Netanya and Herzliah continue to attract Europeans and Americans alike, often with the buyer's eye focused on eventual retirement there.

When you saw the word *abroad* in this chapter's title, you probably already knew where you'd head if you could buy overseas. There is no how-to-select-a-country guide in this chapter, so you should know already what you want your getaway area to be.

WHAT TO LOOK FOR—AND WATCH OUT FOR

Foreign is exciting, different, challenging. It is also, well, *foreign*—alien. You will find some of the differences charming, others irritating. This applies to English-speaking countries as well as those whose principal language is not English.

Here are some points to ponder as you consider flying or driving off into some other land's sunset.

Private American Citizens Residing Abroad

Here is a sampling of countries where Americans might want vacation homes (not every country and not every major city within a country responded to this survey). The numbers below represent full- and part-time residents. They do not include U.S. government (military and nonmilitary) employees and their dependents.

Bahamas	7,600	Ireland	35,000
Bermuda	3,105	Italy	121,000
Canada	422,035	Jamaica	5,200
Costa Rica	19,000	Mexico	453,500
Fiji	4,495	Portugal	8,143
France	48,057	Spain	49,800
Greece	67,000	United Kingdom	215,530
Honduras	11,500		

Source: U.S. Department of State
Based on Reports from U.S. Foreign Service
Posts Received in Fiscal Year 1994

ECONOMICS AND POLITICS

You'll want to know something of the economic health of the nation that interests you. Runaway inflation, double-digit unemployment—every aspect of a nation's economy can affect your realty investment over the long term and could make selling your home difficult if not impossible. Even small economic tremors become important when you own a slice of real estate in a country and are not merely vacationing there.

Take a magnifying glass to the political situation, too. You won't be voting there, but who's in and who's out politically could not only affect your investment but might also spoil your vacations. Even a small uprising that is quickly cooled down can make the evening news at home and leave an unfavorable impression with prospective homebuyers for years to come. And in the event of a "skirmish," what will that country's attitude be toward Americans—and American property?

Who will tell you what's what? You can try several sources for information about the political and economic situation and for answering other questions you will have about living abroad some of the time:

- The embassy in Washington, D.C., of the country that interests you and the American embassy in that country's capital can provide some information, although not much. They will probably have booklets on some aspects of living there. However, even though they can answer a question or two, embassy staff members are not likely to be able to spare the time, and indeed are not likely to have the information, to guide you through a foreign realty purchase.
- If there is an American language newspaper, magazine or newsletter in that country, buy it and study it. Have a subscription delivered to your home before you make your real estate purchase there. Read everything—advertisements included—to get a flavor of how life there really is.
- Ask at the embassy, or perhaps at the American chamber of commerce in the city nearest where you plan to buy, if there is an American colony nearby, or some American professional, trade or social associations. The people you ask will usually provide you with solid information and are often eager to assist a potential American resident.

EXPLORING AN OVERSEAS ADDRESS

Here are some questions to ask yourself when seriously thinking about that vacation spot outside America.

- Will you really want to go there for every vacation? Will you feel guilty if sometimes you'd rather head elsewhere?

- Can you afford to visit as often as you like? Airfares for four, for example, can cost several thousand dollars round-trip. How many trips can you swing? Will one stay annually be enough for you?
- Have you stayed in that country before—in a house or apartment? Being coddled in a hotel for a one-week vacation doesn't count. Rent an apartment or house for a couple of weeks, preferably a month, or try swapping yours for one of theirs (see Chapter 4). Get out and buy groceries, receive mail, make some long-distance phone calls, cook some meals and perhaps deal with plumbers, electricians, exterminators, television (if it's there), repairpersons and others who are part of your life at home. In general, try to live as if you are a resident. You might find it a lot harder than staying in a hotel, perhaps even arduous. Or you might take to it so easily you soon start chatting away like a native.
- Planning to retire there one day? You will want to look into tax benefits for retirees there.

Just Say No

In a 1995 Ann Landers column, a reader complained that she and her husband were being inundated by friends and relatives asking to use the couple's *pied-à-terre* in "a popular European city." The couple intended to spend a few months there every spring (April in Paris?), but then wanted to lock up the flat and disconnect appliances and services. They did *not* want to arrive there each year to face a pile of soiled sheets and towels and malfunctioning appliances. What to do without being impolite?

Ann Landers replied: "Simply say: 'So many close friends and family members have asked that we've decided to say no to everyone. We hope you understand.' P.S. Don't feel guilty. This is a pretty nervy request."

LET'S TALK REAL ESTATE

You've taken the living-in-a-private-home test and have passed triumphantly. You *can* live there, even for just a few weeks each year. You really want to buy now. Here are some tips before you head for the local version of a real estate agent.

Rather important to know: Can you buy where you want? Some countries do not allow real estate purchases by foreigners or do not permit them in specific areas—within a certain distance of the coast, for example, or in historic sections. In Honduras, foreigners are limited to the purchase of no more than three-quarters of an acre of land, and if they are planning to build a home, they must begin construction within three years following their purchase.

There could be other restrictions on purchases. In London, for example, a sizable area of the best residential blocks is owned by the Duke of Westminster and his family. In those blocks one must take a long-term lease on an apartment or house because it is not possible to buy property outright. That lease, with "rent" going to the duke and his family, is a form of ownership.

Are housing prices within your range of affordability? Poke around at agents' offices, read a newspaper's classified and display advertisements, and talk to some Americans and employees of American businesses and offices in the foreign country. You will want to be sure you know what expenses go along with a price quoted, such as real estate taxes and any other charges.

In late 1995, *International Living* analyzed a variety of countries for readers interested in purchasing a retirement home. Their around-the-world checking focused on the price of an average two-bedroom apartment or house in a reasonably good location with electricity, running water and no need for renovation. The winners were ranked in terms of most affordable to most costly.

The top draws in the most affordable category were Ireland, where attractive cottages could be found for $21,000–$22,000, and Ecuador, where a charming two-bedroom, two-bathroom apartment in an attractive residential neighborhood was priced at $35,000. Other lower-costing spots: Belize, Honduras, France and Mexico.

At the other end of the spectrum, the most costly real estate the publication studied turned out to be in New Zealand and Israel. Two-bedroom apartments in New Zealand ranged from $150,000 to $269,000. A two-bedroom town house in Epsom, New Zealand, was, at the time of the survey, priced for sale at $305,000. In Israel, a two-bedroom apartment in Tel Aviv costs up to $600,000. The *International Living* survey found that outside Tel Aviv prices dipped a bit: apartments ranged from $165,000 to $270,000 and houses from $200,000 to $300,000. Other expensive countries are Canada and Thailand.

Countries somewhere in the middle from a real estate perspective were Greece, where a two-bedroom apartment near the beach could be purchased for $82,000, and Spain, where a two-bedroom condo on the Costa del Sol is just under $75,000.

It is unlikely you will want to go as far as Ecuador, New Zealand or other long-distance spots for a second home, but the prices discussed above should give you a general idea of housing costs abroad; and perhaps your country of choice appears in the *International Living* survey.

Be sure the community that attracts you has good roads, good hospitals, good telephone service—basic requirements you might not think of when you are seduced by majestic mountain views, splashes of bougainvillea, the sound of the surf or whatever it is that is drawing you to that dreamy locale on holiday.

If you find a bargain "fixer-upper," learn how the renovation will be handled. What is the bureaucratic process *vis-à-vis* home remodeling there like? Easy? A nightmare? Are workers and building materials readily available? Are construction methods radically different from those here? Is your home accessible? What is the renovation likely to cost? And where will an improvement loan come from?

Your vacation home might come furnished. If it doesn't, are you prepared to furnish it fully, which is especially important if you plan to rent it some of the time? Does the community that interests you have at least a few furniture and home furnishings stores?

If you choose a house or an apartment in a house, who will maintain your home when you are not there? Perhaps you can work out an arrangement with a local real estate company or you might meet and make friends with enough people on your first vacation who can undertake that job for you. If your home is going to be empty for many months, someone must keep an eye on the place. Thinking about maintenance and its attendant problems could steer you to a condominium purchase, where exterior upkeep is, of course, taken care of by the condominium association.

What about rentals? Many buyers of second-home properties abroad are convinced they can earn back those airfares and other expenses attached to their holiday by renting their house or apartment when they aren't there. Is this realistic for you? Take a very businesslike look at the country and neighborhood that interests you. Don't listen to developers and real estate agents who insist you can rent the place 50 weeks a year, no problem. Ask them for papers showing you exactly what properties have been rented, for how long and at what rental rate. Ask, too, what the agency fees for long-distance renting will cost you.

Um . . . Où est . . . um . . . l'Ambassade Américaine?

Somewhere along your path to foreign real estate investment, you will undoubtedly be advised to register with the American embassy or consulate nearest your vacation home. This can be important for a number of reasons, not the least of which is that one of these offices should have your address and phone number in case of a family or business emergency at home.

The embassy or consulate office also takes down your passport information so that if you lose that important document, a new one can be issued with a minimum of fuss.

Mortgages, Titles and Such

The homebuying process in a foreign country will be similar in many ways to buying in this country: You make an offer and it is accepted, perhaps after some haggling. Then you pay cash for your home or secure a mortgage and there is a closing. You are handed the keys to your new place, and voilà! you are a second-home owner and in a foreign country to boot.

That's pretty much it, but you will be surprised at the differences in procedures along the way. Real estate agents, for example, will likely charge a higher commission than the 6 percent that is usual here (paid by the seller, of course). Closing costs for your home can be 15 percent versus the 3 to 6 percent you are used to paying when purchasing American real estate.

You will have to secure a mortgage in your foreign country, not here. (However, you might apply for a loan at a branch of an American bank there if there is one.) You are apt to find lenders willing to extend you a loan for just 50 percent of the purchase price, too, which means you will have to come up with a higher down payment than you might have planned to make.

Sometimes, as in Mexico, every legal document attached to a sale must be executed before a notary public, whose fee can be $3,000 or more. Many countries will charge you a transfer tax or stamp tax with a real estate transfer of property, which can cost a few hundred dollars.

Your real estate agent should be able to explain the buying process to you, but it wouldn't hurt to ask: "How is the down payment/closing/final walk-through handled here?" You don't want any surprises on the road to second-home ownership abroad.

Title is very important in the transfer of property, but it is a part of closing on a home that is not given much emphasis in the states. Here you pay for a title search, a fee that is included in your closing costs, and it is recommended that you purchase title insurance in case a claim to the house by someone else is made in the future.

Treat title more seriously abroad, suggests Jane Lears. "Title problems can be significant," she points out. "In France, for example, some properties are passed on through inheritance. The home you want to buy could be owned by a number of different family members. They all have to sign off that piece of real estate. In some countries you can get title insurance, in others you can't."

Finally, if you want to buy land on which to build, you will want to read Chapter 8, "Buying Land and Building a Home."

Eventually, the i's will be dotted and the t's crossed and your foreign home will be yours. The words you did not understand, the few missteps you took on the road to buying, all have now become part of your introduction to your new part-time home, helping make the settling-in process easier (and providing some interesting dinner party conversation, too). It's exciting and exhilarating to own property abroad.

Congratulations, you sophisticated traveler you!

FOR MORE INFORMATION

The U.S. Department of State offers a number of free booklets for those considering living overseas or those already part-time or full-time residents in another country. One is *Tips for Americans Residing Abroad*, available at U.S. Government Printing Office bookstores, or by writing the Superintendent of Documents, U.S. Government Printing Office, Washington, D.C. 20402. You might also ask for a list of State Department publications.

International Living is published monthly by Agora, Inc., 105 W. Monument St., Baltimore, MD 21201 410-223-2611. The subscription rate for new subscribers is $34 for the first year and $58 each year thereafter.

Some "Try-Before-You-Buy" Resources

Try before you buy through swapping (see Chapter 4) is a truly practical philosophy. Here is another option. Hundreds of rental agencies all over the world specialize in holiday apartments, villas, chateaux and other exotic properties. Unlike travel agencies, most do not accept credit cards, many are likely to want a deposit with your reservation and full payment no later than 45 days before arrival, and some charge a booking fee. If you're satisfied and decide eventually to buy in a particular foreign locale, you may want to turn your new property over to a rental agency to rent when you're not using it. Here are some agencies you might contact:

Bahamas
Abaco Vacation Reservations: 800-633-9197, 508-874-5595, fax 508-874-6308

Island Connections: 919-477-8914, fax 919-477-1019

Caribbean
The Anguilla Connection: 800-916-3336, 809-497-4403, fax 809-497-4402

Antigua Small Properties (Antigua, Montserrat, Barbuda, Nevis): 508-385-4306, fax 508-385-4306

Caribbean Destinations: 800-888-0897, 504-888-7026, fax 504-888-3721

Caribbean Villas & Resorts: 800-338-0987, 207-871-1673

Culebra Island Vacations (Puerto Rico): 800-440-0070, 809-742-3171

Down Island Villa Rentals (Grenada, Grenadines): 800-443-8182, fax 809-443-7086

Four Seasons Villas & Travel (Barbados, St. Lucia, St. Martin, Jamaica): 800-338-0474, 617-639-1055, fax 617-631-8718

San Juan Vacations (Puerto Rico): 800-468-9198, 809-727-1591, fax 809-268-3604

Travel Solutions (British Virgin Islands): 800-832-4509, phone and fax 212-439-0886

Villa Holidays (various Caribbean locales and Mexico): 800-457-0444, 914-937-6944, fax 914-937-7069

Europe & Other International Addresses

Barclay International Group: 800-845-6636, 212-832-3777, fax 212-753-1139

Castles, Cottages, and Flats (England, Ireland, Scotland, France, Italy, and Spain): 800-742-6030, 617-742-6030, fax 617-367-4521

Country Cottages (England, Ireland, Scotland, Wales, France): 800-674-8883, 407-395-5618, fax 407-395-9785

La Cure (Europe, Mexico, Morocco, Caribbean): 800-387-2726, 416-968-2374, fax 416-968-2374

Europa-Let: 800-462-4486, 503-482-5806, fax 503-482-0660

Four Seasons Villas & Travel (England, Scotland, Wales): 800-338-0474, 617-639-1055, fax 617-631-8718

The French Experience: 212-986-1115, fax 212-986-3808

Home at First (England, Scotland, Ireland, Wales): 800-523-5842, 610-543-4348

International Lodging Corporation (Portugal, Spain): 800-772-4644, 212-228-5900, fax 212-677-1815

Italian Villa Rentals: 206-827-3694, fax 206-827-5125

Prestige Villages (Europe, west coast of Mexico, Caribbean): 800-336-0080, 203-254-1302, fax 203-254-7261

Rent A Home International (Europe, Mexico, Caribbean): 800-488-7368, 206-789-9377, fax 206-789-9379

Resorts Management (France, Caribbean, French Polynesia): 800-225-4255, 212-696-4566, fax 212-689-1598

Suzanne T. Pidduck Rentals (Italy, France, Portugal, Spain): 800-726-6702, 805-987-5278, fax 805-482-7976

Swiss Touring (Switzerland): phone and fax 414-963-2010

Twelve Islands and Beyond (Greece, Turkey): 800-345-8236, 202-537-3549, fax 202-537-3549

Villa Leisure (England, south of France, Portugal, Spain, Caribbean): 800-526-4244, 407-624-9000, fax 407-622-9097

Villas of Distinction (south of France, Portugal, Spain, Caribbean): 800-289-0900, 914-273-3331, fax 914-273-3387

Mexico

At Home in Cozumel & Belize (Cozumel, Playa del Carmen, Isla Mujeras, Belize) 800-833-5971, 212-254-5623, fax 212-979-2993

Caribbean Fantasy (Akumal): 800-523-6618, 970-663-2299, fax 970-669-0707

Cozumel Vacation Villas: 303-442-0258, fax 303-442-0380

The World's Top Retirement Havens, published by the editors of *International Living,* is a 240-page paperback book discussing in detail 22 countries from the Bahamas to Venezuela and what life in each is like. Cost is $14.95 plus $2 for shipping and handling. Write *International Living* at its address on page 70.

KEEP IN MIND

➤ Be as informed as possible about the stability of the economy and the political situation in the country you are considering. Or at least be aware that you might be in for a roller-coaster ride there as a resident.

➤ Rent an apartment or house, or swap your home for someone else's there, before you invest in real estate in a foreign country.

➤ Real estate transactions will vary from slightly to substantially different from those in this country.

➤ Look for Americans living in the country (preferably the same city or town) that interests you who can answer questions the guidebooks don't often raise.

PART THREE

What's In and What's Not: A Look at Popular Second-Home Destinations

CHAPTER 10

Following the Lure
of the Sun

Warm winters. Lazy and romantic summers. Mint juleps. Miles of empty beaches. These are some of the traditional images of the American South—images that have long lured folks who can stand only so much winter. Lush golf courses. Posh condominiums. Walt Disney World and all manner of other theme parks. Space shuttle launches. International tourism. The 1996 Summer Olympic Games. These are the modern images of the South.

With the development of railroads, Florida became the first choice of what has become America's Sun Belt. Gilded age millionaires who could have built palaces wherever they pleased turned the Sunshine State from a sleepy backwater to a winter playground for high society—and later for the rest of us. According to the U.S. Travel Data Center, some 50 percent of respondents to a survey on preferred winter destinations still choose Florida, and it remains the Sun Belt's top vacation state. It is also the first choice of leisure-home buyers, especially those with eventual retirement in mind.

Still, Florida is not the only game in town. That original southern escape has become the Sun Belt escape, as shivering northerners and, increasingly, Europeans vacation there. Developers have sprinkled vacation communities across the country from Palm Beach to Palm Springs, creating vast choices for homebuyers. Some are snowbirds, who visit every year and want a Sun Belt getaway to call their own. Others never want to live in colder climes again.

Batter Up

In every major league city, except Denver, baseball attendance has taken on the trajectory of a well-pitched sinker. However, spring training really packs in the fans across the Sun Belt. Regardless of league, all East Coast and most midwestern teams play in Florida; some midwestern teams and all but one western team, in Arizona. Pitchers report for training camp in early February, and games begin late in the month and in early March, continuing until the start of the regular season. Here's where to find your favorite team, plus phone numbers for schedules and ticket information:

Team	Spring Training	Phone
American League		
Baltimore Orioles	Fort Lauderdale, FL	954-776-1921
Boston Red Sox	Fort Myers, FL	941-334-4700
California Angels	Phoenix, AZ	602-784-4444
Chicago White Sox	Sarasota, FL	941-954-7669
Cleveland Indians	Winter Haven, FL	941-293-3900
Detroit Tigers	Lakeland, FL	941-499-8229
Kansas City Royals	Davenport, FL	941-424-2500
Milwaukee Brewers	Chandler, AZ	602-895-6000
Minnesota Twins	Fort Myers, FL	800-33-TWINS
New York Yankees	Tampa, FL	813-879-1523
Oakland Athletics	Phoenix, AZ	602-392-0217
Seattle Mariners	Peoria, AZ	602-412-9008
Texas Rangers	Port Charlotte, FL	941-625-9500
Toronto Blue Jays	Dunedin, FL	813-733-0429
National League		
Atlanta Braves	West Palm Beach, FL	407-683-6100
Chicago Cubs	Mesa, AZ	602-964-4467
Cincinnati Reds	Plant City, FL	813-752-7337
Colorado Rockies	Tucson, AZ	520-327-9467
Florida Marlins	Melbourne, FL	407-633-9200
Houston Astros	Kissimmee, FL	407-839-3900
Los Angeles Dodgers	Vero Beach, FL	407-569-6858
Montreal Expos	West Palm Beach, FL	407-684-6801
New York Mets	Port St. Lucie, FL	407-871-2115
Philadelphia Phillies	Clearwater, FL	813-442-8496
Pittsburgh Pirates	Bradenton, FL	941-748-4610
St. Louis Cardinals	St. Petersburg, FL	813-894-4773
San Diego Padres	Peoria, AZ	602-486-7000
San Francisco Giants	Scottsdale, AZ	602-990-7972

THE FLORIDA PHENOMENON

Florida tops just about every wish list for winter escapes and second-home purchases. This is not surprising, given the fact that it's the East Coast's largest and most varied state. The distance from Jacksonville in the northeastern corner to Key West, which is, in spirit, a Caribbean island, is nearly 500 miles. And Pensacola, on the western tip of the Panhandle, is more than 350 miles from Jacksonville, even in a different time zone. Generous Atlantic beaches, vibrant Miami, the sparkling Florida Keys, the increasingly popular west coast communities with the Gulf of Mexico at their front doors, the surprising Panhandle and central Florida with its mix of Disney action and agricultural tranquility provide everything you could wish for except mountains, of course.

The Upper East Coast

You can travel the eastern coast of Florida quickly by interstate highway, in a more leisurely fashion on subsidiary roads that parallel the coastline or by boat along the Intracoastal Waterway. If you are coming from the Northeast, Jacksonville might well be your main port of entry. Located in northeastern Florida, this city of one million is temperate and pleasant year-round, but just because it's in Florida, don't think it's the tropics. It's a city with kinship to upcoast Georgia and the Carolinas, where summer is, well, summery, and winters are moderate to cool.

Did You Know. . .

. . . that Jacksonville is the largest city in the continental United States in terms of land mass? It spreads over 840 square miles of woodland, riverside and shore.

Jacksonville is a practical, functional city with a generous port and a thriving, if scattered, business culture. Jacksonville Landing, a well-designed shopping and entertainment complex on the St. John River, is a modern mecca. The past still lives in Fernandina Beach, a nearby Victorian jewel. Golf is great at nearby Sawgrass and Amelia Island Plantation, and the beaches are terrific from here all the way down to Miami.

Just south of Jacksonville you'll find St. Augustine, a delightful and historic city. In 1513, Ponce de Leon led an expedition to what is now northeastern Florida and found the alleged Fountain of Youth. Half a century before the Pilgrims set foot on Plymouth Rock, the Florida site was colonized as the first permanent European settlement in the New World. It was also an early vacation-home destination when millionaires' mansions began appearing in the old city.

St. Augustine's heart still beats to a historical rhythm. Tourists flock to the Castillo de San Marcos, a 17th-century Spanish fortress; to the Fountain of Youth Historical Park; and to the oldest house, oldest store and oldest wooden schoolhouse in the United States. They stroll along St. George Street in the heart of old St. Augustine and hop aboard a sightseeing boat to cruise the scenic waterfront and Matanzas Bay. St. Augustine now anchors booming leisure-oriented communities that attract northern snowbirds during the winter, vacationing families in the summer and retirees year-round.

Did You Know. . .

. . . that some 40 million visitors come to Florida each year, and about 30 million of them go to Walt Disney World?

Continuing south, Daytona Beach is the next major city. It has a fortuitous location, roughly equidistant from St. Augustine, Orlando and Cape Canaveral. It also boasts "the most famous beach in the world," a sparkling strip of white sand 500 feet wide and 23 miles long. If you're a northerner accustomed to beach signs forbidding all sorts of beach activities from diving to littering to bringing glass containers to the beach, you'll be stunned to see people driving vehicles across the sand.

Beach driving is part Florida custom and part Daytona heritage. In the early days of tourism and automobiles, R. E. Olds (as in Oldsmobile) and Henry Ford used to drive up and down in front of the Ormond Hotel as part of their sales efforts. In 1928, a dapper Englishman named Malcolm Campbell gunned a home-made vehicle over the sand at nearly 207 miles an hour (he later achieved 272 MPH), becoming a local hero. You may still drive on the beach, but 10 miles an hour is the limit. If you seek speed, check out the Daytona 500 in mid-February, or the Firecracker 400 or the Paul Revere 250, both in July.

Is there anyone who doesn't feel as if he or she has actually been to Cape Canaveral? No matter how often we've seen them televised, shuttle launches still have the power to make us feel as if we too are shooting for the stars. In a state where the created environments of theme parks are significant attractions, how refreshing to find one with authentic roots and ongoing functions. The Kennedy Space Center puts on a fascinating spectacle, and witnessing a liftoff or landing will send shivers down your spine. For recorded information, call 407-452-2121. If you're a space junkie, you may wish to explore property in nearby Cocoa Beach, though Cape Canaveral is certainly an easy commute from Daytona or Orlando.

Did You Know. . .

. . . that the Lely Flamingo Club, designed by Robert Trent Jones, Sr., is Naples' only public signature golf course?

Orlando has become Florida's epicenter. If you're vacationing, it will certainly be on your itinerary, and if you're considering buying a place in the Sunshine State, you at least need to take a look at this boomtown and its neighbors. The mighty engine of Walt Disney World (the Magic Kingdom, Epcot, and Disney-MGM Studios) drives visitation to central Florida.

Cypress Gardens in nearby Winter Haven predated the Disney deluge by decades and really started the theme park business, and its flower-filled acreage, sparkling lake and other attractions are still worthwhile. Other "themeries," closer to the Disney complex have followed: Sea World of Florida, Universal Studios Florida, Wet 'n Wild and other amusements. If you've even thought about vacationing with kids or grandkids, you've probably already explored greater Orlando's myriad attractions, and because so many like-minded tourists do so, it remains a top Sun Belt real estate hotspot.

When you peel the little "Indian River" sticker off your citrus fruit, you're removing the tag applied to it somewhere along a quiet, hundred-mile stretch of coastal wonder roughly halfway between St. Augustine and Palm Beach. Vero Beach, Fort Pierce, Port St. Lucie and Jupiter Beach are the prime communities in Indian River country. For vacationers and leisure-home buyers, it's an area of contrasts, with both sublime and achievable destinations. Hobe Sound falls into the sublime category. While not the flashiest, this is one of Florida's most enduringly exclusive communities. By contrast, Club Med, whose philosophy is steeped in egalitarianism, selected nearby Port St. Lucie for its Sandpiper Village, the first in America's Sun Belt. Indian River Plantation north of Stuart started out as a condominium community and has blossomed into a fine golf and maritime resort that attracts vacationers and homebuyers alike.

South Florida and the Keys

As you continue southward, you'll finally reach the region where winter is virtually nonexistent—just a chilly memory for emigrés from the snow zone but unknown to natives.

First you come to Fort Lauderdale, a big, brassy town that has worked hard to shed the nonstop beach-party image created by a generation of spring-breaking college students. Fort Lauderdale's fantastic seven-mile beach that lured those students is still there and so is an intracity waterway system that has earned Fort Lauderdale the nickname "Venice of America," the northernmost reef diving on the Atlantic seaboard, a new arts center and an attractive oceanfront walkway. Legions of snowbirds escaping winter in the North populate high-rise condo buildings overlooking the Atlantic. If cruising is your thing, chances are pretty good that you'll eventually embark from Fort Lauderdale's impressive ship terminal.

Did You Know. . .

. . . that Florida is the epitome of a booming state?

The next stop is Palm Beach, which is located in what is now known as Florida's Gold Coast, a chain of sparkling communities between Fort Lauderdale and Miami. Henry Flagler "ran" his railroad to Palm Beach, and a visionary named Addison Mizner developed a hybrid and very opulent architectural style—sort of a romanticized Moorish-Gothic-Romanesque—in neighboring Boca Raton. The lions of High Society flocked to the Gold Coast to build astonishing mansions. Although the first big real estate boom of the 1920s went bust during the depression, the benign climate, stylish residential neighborhoods, expensive shops and overall glamour have never gone out of fashion.

Miami is the Sun Belt's most international city. It has emerged from its reputation as a haven for northern retirees into the hip locale of *Miami Vice* and, increasingly, as the gateway to Latin America and the playground for Central and South American visitors. Along with Miami Beach, a separate city located across Biscayne Bay, and such communities as Coral Gables, Coconut Grove, Key Biscayne and Bal Harbour, greater Miami translates into a culturally rich and vibrant metropolitan area. The lovingly restored and ultrastylish Art Deco buildings of South Beach at the southern end of Miami Beach have become a mecca for the hip and trendy.

James Deering, whose fortune came from International Harvester, built Villa Vizcaya, an art-filled Renaissance-style palace that is now a museum. Even more than the other sumptuous manors dotting the coast, it demonstrates what millionaires *used* to think a vacation home should be.

Did You Know. . .

. . . that of the 14,000 golf courses in the United States, more than 1,000 are in Florida?

"The Best Golf Courses in Florida" is a CD-ROM depicting 106 of the state's top 10 percent. Locations of and driving directions to 106 courses, their ratings, greens fees, cart rental fees, even course layouts and pictures are available on this visually interesting and informational disk. It's $24.95 by calling 800-705-9945.

Families love the nearby Museum of Science and Planetarium as well as the Seaquarium, the Miami Youth Museum, the Parrot Jungle where some thousand parrots, toucans and macaws roost, and the Monkey Jungle where people are restrained and simians roam free. Within a 40-mile radius of Miami there will be, by the time you read this, about 50 golf courses. The city is also the gateway to the Everglades, a timeless, magical 2,000-square-mile wilderness area of swamps, wetlands and islands.

The Florida Keys point like a staccato saber toward Cuba. "Key" is a corruption of the Spanish word *cayo*, which means reef or island.

Although these small islands are connected to the mainland and each other via an artery, they are spiritually apart. Residents think of themselves as being of the Keys rather than of the mainland, and it won't take you long to feel that way too.

Origin of International Visitors

If you are considering buying a leisure home that you might also want to rent out when you are not using it, burgeoning inbound tourism from other countries is a factor to consider. In recent years, nearly one in six foreign tourists has visited Florida. Here's the breakdown:

Area of Origin	U.S. Overall (total 35.8 million)	Florida (total 6 million)
Canada	41.8%	30.7%
Europe	23.7	30.9
Asia	16.4	2.4
South America	6.0	18.8
Central America	1.5	3.8
Mexico	4.6	3.9
Caribbean	2.8	7.9
Other	3.2	1.6

U.S. Travel & Tourism Administration, 1994 figures

A drive to Key West along the 113-mile chain of roadways and bridges officially known as the Overseas Highway takes you over a shimmering salt sea and past some of the Key's leading landmarks: Key Largo, location of the namesake Bogie-Bacall movie; Key Vaca at the midpoint of the archipelago; and Big Pine Key, the last refuge of a herd of tiny Key deer. Key West is Florida's Provincetown—the picturesque, arty, literary and slightly outrageous community literally at the end of the road.

The West Coast

If Miami is Florida's liveliest and Key West its most creative, the state's image mellows as you proceed northward up the west coast. You come first to the Lee Island Coast, the western gateway to the Everglades. Thomas Edison and Henry Ford built winter homes there that you can now tour. Cape Coral, the region's largest city, boasts more miles of canals than Venice, while the namesake of another Italian city, Naples, draws executives and tycoons.

Nearby Fort Myers, the southernmost Civil War battle site, has established itself as a retirement mecca. It is also the springboard to a group of enchanting islands known for their pristine beaches and laid-back, family-friendly ambiance. Sanibel especially and Captiva to an extent yield more than 400 species of sensational shells that wash ashore with each tide. Peak shelling season is May to October, and "Sanibel stoop" is local lingo for describing shellers' posture as they beachcomb for desirable mollusks. The 5,000-acre J.N. "Ding" Darling National Wildlife Refuge preserves tidal estuaries, wetlands and mangroves, which serve as the habitat of raccoons, otters, alligators and birds, The nearby 1,100-acre Sanibel-Captiva Conservation Foundation contains a high ground where tortoises, more birds and even a few bobcats have been seen.

Did You Know. . .

. . . that Florida's most populous county is Dade (where Miami is) with more than 2.1 million residents, and its least populous is Lafayette with roughly 6,000 (located inland, in the crook between the peninsula and the Panhandle).

In addition to nature lovers, preretirees seeking moderate prices, miles of outstanding beach, 95 golf courses, 58 marinas, fabulous fishing and the exceptional Mann Performing Arts Hall also appreciate the overall congenial Lee Island Coast lifestyle. Before he retreated to Hawaii, Charles Lindbergh used to vacation on Sanibel, and Anne Morrow Lindbergh's *Gifts from the Sea* was set there, though she did not identify the island in her best-selling book.

The middle part of the coast offers a concentration of inviting communities. Tampa is a big city with high-rise office towers, colleges and leisure-oriented communities known for great golf and other diversions. A section called Ybor City marches to a distinctly Latin beat and is America's cigar-making capital, and therefore the hub of a revitalized growth industry. Across the bay is the retirement Eden of St. Petersburg, noteworthy for its enormous acreage devoted to parks and public recreation areas. Treasure Island, Clearwater Beach, Bellair Beach, Madeira Beach and Redington Beach are among the region's relaxing shore communities, while Innisbrook in Tarpon Springs draws legions of golf and tennis aficionados.

Shop 'till You Drop; Buy 'till You Die

New York has Fifth Avenue. Beverly Hills has Rodeo Drive. Here are half a dozen of Florida's most noteworthy shopping streets:

City	Shopping Street
Fort Lauderdale	Las Olas Boulevard
Miami	Lincoln Road
Naples	Third Street
Palm Beach	Worth Avenue
Sarasota	St. Armand's Circle
Winter Park	Park Avenue

The Florida Panhandle is where vacationers are largely drive-in visitors from Alabama, Mississippi, Louisiana and Texas. In fact, it has irreverently and affectionately been nicknamed the "Redneck Riviera." Southern families are happy to find a friendly welcome and moderate prices. Fishing, canoeing in clear rivers and catching some rays are the typical Panhandle visitor's answer to all that glittery golf and tense tennis. There's also a ghostly glimmer of the elegant Old South, exemplified in "time-stood-still" Pensacola, the state's westernmost city.

With more than 13 million people, Florida is the nation's fourth most populous state after California, New York and Texas. It has also been among the fastest-growing states, increasing more than 13-fold in 75 years and nearly tripling in 35 years. In 1920, Florida had 968,470 residents; in 1930, 1,468,211; in 1940, 1,897,414; in 1950, 2,051,560; in 1960, 4,951,560; in 1970, 6,791,418; and in 1980, 9,746,961. The 1990 census showed 12,937,926 residents, and estimates were for 13,953,000—up over a million—by the end of 1994.

THE GLORIOUS GULF COAST

The Gulf Coast, which extends from the Florida Panhandle to Texas, makes headlines when a hurricane hits or oil spills. But it holds great allure for vacationers and second-home owners who love the sand and the sea, and savor such a rich array of diversions as fishing, hunting and gambling.

Mississippi

People who live nearby have long known about the Gulf. Consider Mississippi's Gulf Coast towns: One-quarter of all visitors are from Louisiana, 20 percent from Florida, 18 percent from elsewhere in-state, 13 percent from Alabama, and 20 percent cumulatively from Georgia, Texas, Tennessee and Missouri. That leaves just 2 percent from the rest of the world. Other Gulf Coast states are similarly undiscovered.

Like the Panhandle itself, the part of the Gulf Coast stretching to New Orleans offers an unhurried getaway—and perhaps the site of *your* ideal vacation home. The Mississippi, Alabama and Louisiana parts are characterized by lively beach resorts and mellow fishing communities etched out of dense lowland forests of scrub oak and slash pine, and thousands upon thousands of islands. It is a complex topograph comprising untold acres of low-lying wetlands. In this picturesque tangle of rivers, marshes, streams, swamps and lakes, mammal, fish and bird species abound.

Art and history abound as well. You can explore numerous historic plantations plus such special attractions as the Walter Anderson Museum of Art in Ocean Springs, Mississippi, which celebrates Gulf landscapes; Bellingrath Gardens 20 miles south of Mobile where spectacular formal gardens were carved from the wild brush; and Beauvoir, the stately home in Biloxi where Jefferson Davis spent his last years.

Mississippi's little stretch of coast is scrunched between Alabama and Louisiana. It is just 63 miles wide, but gambling has thrust it into the big leagues. A dozen Las Vegas-style, 24-hour-a-day casinos in such places as Biloxi, Lakeshore and Bay St. Louis have spurred a boom. This in turn has led some folks to discover the 26 miles of beach within those 63 miles and to flock to more traditional resort towns with the usual assortment of golf (19 courses), tennis and other diversions.

Arkansas

Although Arkansas is not on the coast, it is often considered part of the Gulf region. Until Whitewater, a star-crossed development proposed near Eureka Springs, Arkansas, hit the headlines, few people outside of the South considered the state to be a vacation destination or a place for a vacation home. Located on the northern fringes of the Sun Belt, its early and enduring vacation popularity rests largely on the appeal of Hot Springs. This spa city in south central Arkansas is adjacent to Hot Springs National Park, and its bath houses purvey curative and relaxing waters. The city is also a regional cultural mecca where arts and entertainment flourish. Outdoor lovers treasure the surrounding hilly woodlands and lakes for hiking and water sports in a lovely setting.

Did You Know. . .

. . . that the federal government has administered 47 springs in and around Hot Springs, Arkansas, since 1832, elevating them to national park status in 1921?

Texas

To out-of-staters, Texas always seems larger than life. And so it should. This beefy state, the largest of the lower 48, covers 262,017 square miles in two time zones and ranges in elevation from sea level to the 8,749-foot summit of Guadalupe Peak. Its landscape changes from region to region: plantation-style fields of cotton, rice and sugarcane in the east, citrus groves in the south, arid plains and prairie in the north and west, and both arid land and high mountains in the Pecos River and Big Bend regions of the southwest. In the major metropolitan areas—Houston, Dallas/Fort Worth and San Antonio—populations are concentrated in sophisticated urban settings. When we think of Texas, it is typically of the Alamo, glittering towers, major-league sports teams and Mission Control. But the hundreds of miles of sandy shoreline along the Gulf Coast offer the most beguiling vacation getaway with the broadest appeal.

While other Texas cities trace their roots to oil exploration, cattle, farming, manufacturing or military history, Galveston on the Gulf thrived as a port, much like some of New England's cities. It remains an important deepwater harbor, but with 32 miles of beachfront set against a charming seaside city, it is also a fine vacation destination. Mardi Gras in February, spring break, and the Galveston Island Shrimp Festival in mid-April are the busiest times.

Another fabulous stretch of Texas sand and sea is Padre Island, roughly halfway between Corpus Christi and Port Isabel. This 113-mile paradise of coastal grasslands and dunes offers miles of pristine beaches for swimming, lazing, windsurfing and surf fishing, while the Grassland Hiking Trail appeals to the restless. Corpus Christi is also the gateway to Port Aransas, a quiet hideaway for vacationers who like to fish, sun and walk for miles on a gorgeous beach.

Did You Know. . .

. . . that 350 species of birds are found on Padre Island?

THE SUN-SATIONAL SOUTHWEST

Georgia O'Keeffe, D. H. Lawrence and other artistic souls were captivated by the southwestern desert in the early years of this century. The rest of us are just catching up. The art, architecture, fabrics, jewelry and cuisine of the Southwest are hot trends. So is the new spirituality that emphasizes human connectedness to the earth. Both have had a mighty influence on fashion, furnishings and lifestyles that have spread across the land. Hispanic and Native American influences are superb matches for the starkly beautiful southwestern desert, and they offer a stylistic escape from the rest of the country.

If you settle on a second home in the Southwest, it might well be in the adobe style that traces its roots to pre-Columbian Indians known as the Anasazi. You'll probably put Navajo rugs on Mexican tile floors, sit down at a Spanish mission-style table, invest in some really good pottery, hang a chili-pepper *ristra* in your kitchen and learn to whip a mean kettle of *posole*.

New Mexico

Albuquerque, New Mexico's capital and largest city, is a major center of southwestern style. Fast-growing and energetic, it offers outstanding desert-and-mountain scenery, youthful energy from the University of New Mexico campus and the striking Anglo-Hispanic-Native American cultural mix. It is also the jumping-off point for Santa Fe, Taos and several Indian pueblos to the north. Both Santa Fe and Taos enjoy status as art centers. Both have enough radiant, year-round sun to qualify as Sun Belt meccas; but with its higher elevation, winter carries a nip in the air and the surrounding mountains offer excellent skiing.

Ruidoso in the southern part of the state is primarily a summer playground of pine-covered mountains, the cooling waters of Rio Bonito and Rio Ruidoso, fine golf courses and insights into our past. The newly enlarged American Museum of the Horse is one of the most interesting specialty museums in the country. This is Billy the Kid country as well, and it continues to draw western history buffs who want to see where the youthful outlaw alternately eluded and battled the authorities in 1877–78.

Alamogordo's legacy includes the geological and the technological. The White Sands National Monument is a gleaming 300-square-mile basin whose stark and dramatic beauty is worth a visit. Many people who visit do so less for the terrain than to pay homage to the rocket test site—White Sands Proving Ground—where the world's first atomic blast took place on July 16, 1945. Another attraction is Alamagordo's Space Center with the International Space Hall of Fame and related attractions. Angel Fire and Cloudcroft, two of the country's southernmost ski areas, make this region a year-round destination.

Arizona

Florida's closest rival as a Sun Belt destination is Arizona. It's the one you'll prefer if you like a desert climate better than a coastal one. The Grand Canyon State is growing fast: From Flagstaff in the north to Tucson not far from the Mexican border, the desert is abloom with new subdivisions, golf courses and services. Phoenix and neighboring Scottsdale epitomize this growth. They have mushroomed and melded into a major metropolitan area in the heart of the state. People love the mild winters, excellent golf and desert scenery spreading gorgeously from the Superstition Mountains.

The Sonora Desert Museum and the Pima County Air Museum are big draws in Tucson, southern Arizona's fast-growing city. Three new 18-hole golf courses were added in 1995–96 alone to fill the demand. Sedona, a jewel of a town in the midst of stunning redrock country north of Phoenix, is an art colony and New Age center.

But the real Arizona lies beyond the city lights. The state is suffused with stark natural beauty. Flagstaff is the main gateway to the canyon that draws millions of annual visitors—the Grand Canyon. Most peer over its rim and invade its gift shops, but, in truth, you can spend days exploring and photographing the hidden corners of this dramatically beautiful state. The Petrified Forest and Saguaro National Monument are other compelling Arizona natural attractions. The Hopi and Navajo are immensely creative people. Their jewelry, pottery, rugs and other works are sold all over the West and are a major part of the beauty and richness of Arizona.

Did You Know. . .

. . . that so much water is drawn from the Colorado River to irrigate golf courses and lawns in the Phoenix area that the entire valley's microclimate has changed? What was once a bone-dry desert now has measurable humidity, created by water evaporation.

Nevada

The southern tip of Nevada resembles a triangle with a bite taken from it to accommodate Lake Mead. Tucked into this very small section of a very large state are two of the Sun Belt's current boomtowns. Las Vegas, a glittering center for entertainment, gambling and conventioneering, has mushroomed to over a million residents who like the easygoing lifestyle. Where else can you find hotels and entertainment complexes that mimic medieval Europe, Paris, the New York skyline, Polynesia or a circus tent? Here's where neon and artifice take over from earthy adobe but, oh, with what flair it's all done. Although they got their start as adult playgrounds where the "slots" never stop, the city's big hotels are becoming nonstop entertainment centers for families. Laughlin, virtually at the southernmost tip of the tip, has been nicknamed "Little Las Vegas." It is following in big Las Vegas's glamorous footsteps with casino entertainment, but it still comes across as a smaller, more restrained version.

Palm Springs, California

Palm Springs, built around hot mineral springs, experienced its first growth spurt in the 1920s when Hollywood moguls and stars, and their retainers, sought an escape from the southern California coast, which most people think of as a place to go *to* for a holiday rather than a place to escape *from*. Actor Charlie Farrell founded the Racquet Club, which quickly became the place to be seen—and it remained so through the Eisenhower era. Bob Hope, Frank Sinatra, Gerald and Betty Ford, and a myriad of other famous folk started out vacationing in Palm Springs and now make it their primary residence. Sonny Bono, now a U.S. representative, was Palm Springs' mayor from 1988–92. Jennifer Jason Leigh, photographer Annie Leibovitz, Dwight Yoakam, Arnold Schwarzenegger, Ted Danson, and Mary Steenburgen are regulars—or at least occasionals. Stargazing may be a prime visitors' pursuit.

Palm Springs Desert Resorts

Total population	About 200,000
Annual visitors	About 3 million
Golf courses	87
Tennis courts	600
Swimming pools	30,000
Average temperature range	43 to 69 degrees in January, 59 to 91 degrees in April, 76 to 108 degrees in May, 63 to 93 degrees in October (but the thermometer hit a scorching 114 on St. Patrick's Day 1996, when Michael Chang won tennis's Newsweek Cup at Indian Wells)

Palm Springs hit its zenith so long ago and has had such a high proportion of older homeowners that local wags have called it "God's little waiting room." But that is changing, too, as a new generation discovers its charms. In fact, the novel that spawned the term *Generation X* was set in Palm Springs. Some of the world's best golf, incredible shopping, a weekly music and shopping extravaganza called VillageFest, a scenic tram ride, and exploring the San Jacinto, Little San Bernardino, or Santa Rosa Mountains, Indian Canyons, and nearby Joshua Tree National Monument exemplify the variety of diversions in this desert oasis.

Top Scuba Sites

The readers of *Rodale's Scuba Diving* ranked the top five mainland U.S. scuba diving spots as follows:

1. Outer Banks, North Carolina

2. California and Islamorada, Florida Keys (tie)

4. Channel Islands, California

5. Flower Garden Banks, Texas

Where Palm Springs was once *the* California desert town, it has developed into a cluster of communities stretching along Interstate 10 collectively known as Palm Springs Desert Resorts. From east to west, they are Desert Hot Springs, Palm Springs, Cathedral City, Rancho Mirage, Palm Desert, Indian Wells, La Quinta and Indio. Dozens of golf courses blanket the region (celebrity golf tournaments such as the Bob Hope Classic and the Dinah Shore LPGA tournament take place there), which is one of its major draws. Family theme parks, museums, cultural centers, full-scale resorts and residential developments galore round out the picture.

KEEP IN MIND

➤ More people head for the sun than the snow for their leisure time—and with an aging population, that trend is likely to continue.

➤ Florida has been the Sun Belt's most popular vacation (and vacation-home) destination for decades.

➤ Jupiter is roughly the northern end of south Florida. There, the climate begins to change. To the north, you'll probably still need a sweater or light jacket during some winter days. To the south, it's shirtsleeve country.

CHAPTER 11

Magical Mountain Meccas

Skiing and snowboarding are individual but very sociable sports, which people tend to do with family or friends. They can be shared by people of all ages and, in fact, are among those rare activities in which kids, parents and grandparents can participate together. Recognizing that all family members do not downhill ski or snowboard, off-slope activities abound in ski country. North America's leading winter resorts, especially those in the Rocky Mountains, are the peer of the finest on earth, and, in fact, they now attract skiers from all over the world. Full-service resorts, which represent the top tier of the continent's ski areas, offer outstanding terrain plus the full range of resort services: airport pickup, lodging, skiing, ski instruction for adults and children, child care for little ones too young to ski, intra-resort transportation, dining, shopping and entertainment. Eastern and West Coast ski resorts tend to draw more regional business, while the Rockies have more cosmic appeal.

Cross-country skiing, snowshoeing, health and beauty spas, ice skating, horseback riding and sleighrides are just a few of the options at leading ski resorts. They are now becoming summer destinations, too, with golf, hiking, nature walks, tennis and mountain biking along with music, dance and art festivals as top summer draws, giving vacationers an opportunity to get a lay of the land at off-season rates and increasing the rental potential for second-home owners.

Ski Industry: Flat or Fit?

No doubt about it—skier numbers are flat. The number of skiers or snowboarders entering the sport roughly balances those leaving it, and skier visits nationwide have not grown substantially over the last decade and a half. However, today's skiers are willing to spend more on lodging, lift tickets, meals and diversions than their counterparts half a generation ago.

THE ROCKIES

Colorado

What Florida is to sunseekers, Colorado is to skiers: number one by a landslide. America's ski areas tally more than 50 million skier days (each representing one skier or snowboarder on the slopes for a day), and of those, roughly 20 percent are on Colorado mountains. Some of those sliding down Colorado slopes are in-state skiers, mostly day-tripping from Denver, Colorado Springs and other metropolitan areas, but the lion's share are vacationers.

To many skiers, the *crème de la crème* is Vail. Its ski area and the foundation of what was to become the town debuted in 1962. In less than 35 years, Vail grew from a livestock pasture in Colorado's central Rockies to a megaresort promoted as the Vail Valley. Located just two hours west of Denver, it attracts fussy vacationers from all over the world. It is, by most measures, the largest single-mountain ski area in the country with more lift capacity, more skiable acreage and more annual skier visits than any other.

Beaver Creek, ten miles to the west, is Vail's even more upscale sibling. You can ski Vail and Beaver Creek on one fully interchangeable lift ticket, but you can't simply drive to the resort. Unless you are "overnighting," you have to take a bus to one of the few gated resorts in the Rockies. Beaver Creek has set new standards of luxury, with large, lavish condominiums, second homes and upscale timeshares in a bowl-like valley. It's so posh that it even has a resort concierge rather than the traditional skier services desk. This is where former President Gerald Ford has his ski house; you can see the small Secret Service station from the Strawberry Park chairlift. In 1996, a chairlift link was

> ## Western Ski Resorts with Major Conference Centers
>
> If you are interested in buying a place that could rent practically year-round, be aware of the meetings and conference facilities popping up all over North America's mountain towns.
>
> - Beaver Creek, Colorado
> - Big Sky, Montana
> - Keystone, Colorado
> - Snowbird, Utah
> - Snowmass, Colorado
> - Whistler, British Columbia

established between Beaver Creek and Arrowhead, which previously offered small-potatoes skiing and big-time golf, even further improving easy access from both resorts to both sports and making it one of America's largest ski complexes.

Aspen and Vail. Vail and Aspen. This Colorado twosome is generally spoken of in the same breath—like salt and pepper. If Vail epitomizes a built-from-scratch resort that blossomed with success, Aspen is synonymous with a town that has enjoyed the ultimate renaissance. This nineteenth-century silver-mining boomtown all but sank into oblivion by the 1930s. Renaissance came when the first lift was strung up the steep slopes of Aspen Mountain in 1947 and the Goethe Bicentennial was held in the town of Aspen in 1949. These two events, which with half a century of hindsight seem to have occurred simultaneously, formed the substructure on which the most glamorous ski resort in America and one of its leading intellectual and cultural centers was built.

Now four ski areas are accessible by a single lift ticket: the original Aspen Mountain, still one of the continent's most challenging; nearby Buttermilk and Aspen Highlands; and sprawling Snowmass, 12 miles away. Historic Aspen with its glamorized, gentrified downtown core has spread through the valley and up mountainsides with knock-your-socks-off designer homes, condominiums and town houses. Opulent shops, gourmet restaurants, first-rate art galleries often selling museum-quality works and great nightspots make Aspen a scintillating resort town.

Then and Now

Resort development has its "lost-shirt" tales but also its wild success stories. Vail is among the latter. What is now arguably America's foremost ski resort started in 1959 with a big dream and modest capitalization. Twenty-one investors put up $5,000 each to buy a 520-acre ranch at $110 per acre plus minimal equipment to build a resort. To raise the additional $1.8 million needed for construction of the ski area, the fledgling company took out a bank loan and sold 100 limited partnerships at $10,000 each, which included four lifetime passes to the new ski area.

Today, the rock-bottom sticker price for a high-speed quad chairlift is $2 million, with complicated engineering or construction problems additional. Vail and Beaver Creek between them boast 15 such express lifts plus a brand new, $12 million state-of-the-art gondola. During the 1995–96 winter, a one-day adult lift ticket cost $48 and an adult's season ski pass cost $1,500.

In 1995, a new development called Bachelor Gulch went on the market. The buying frenzy of affluent guests, many of whom already owned Vail Valley property, was so intense that a lottery was established to decide who would be permitted to buy. On the first day of the Bachelor Gulch sale, 52 buyers put down $43 million for choice building lots at $425,000 to $1.5 million for each two-acre to four-acre lot.

The Vail tale probably will never be repeated, and start-up investments are at least as risky as they were in the years Eisenhower and Kennedy lived in the White House, but it's worth thinking about if you visit a resort with a ground-floor opportunity.

Second-home owners, past and current, comprise a virtual who's who of contemporary glamour: Hollywood producer Jon Peters, actor Don Johnson, TV performer Vanna White, ex-Playmate Barbi Benton, real estate mogul Donald Trump, former 20th Century Fox chief (and once the owner of the Aspen Skiing Company) Marvin Davis, and a cornucopia of other gossip column names.

Snowmass was launched in the early 1970s as a planned-from-scratch resort with abundant slopeside lodging and excellent ski terrain. In winter, it is one of the world's preeminent ski destinations. In summer, Aspen and Snowmass host the Aspen Institute for Humanistic Studies, Aspen Music Festival, DanceAspen, art workshops at Anderson Ranch Arts Center and lesser-known events.

Did You Know. . .

. . . that Vail and neighboring Beaver Creek are the only resorts to host the prestigious World Alpine Ski Championships more than once, first in 1989 with a reprise scheduled for 1999? The only other American resort to host the World Championships was Aspen in 1950.

Other Colorado mountains may not have the instant name recognition among nonskiers that Vail and Aspen enjoy, but some other mountains are exceptional in their own right. Crested Butte is just 12 miles from Aspen as the proverbial crow flies but up to a four-hour drive along roads that snake between pristine wilderness areas. You'll be captivated by the charm of the old mining town of Crested Butte and the slopeside resort development of Crested Butte Mountain Resort three miles away. The ski terrain ranges from some of Colorado's easiest slopes to some of its steepest, and in summer Crested Butte is a noteworthy mountain-biking mecca.

Summit County, right off Interstate 70, is well under a two-hour drive from Denver. Its four ski areas (Arapahoe Basin, Breckenridge, Copper Mountain and Keystone) and four towns/resort developments (Breckenridge, Dillon, Frisco and Keystone) annually rack up more skier visits than the entire state of Utah. All the ski areas except Copper Mountain are under single ownership and offer a fully interchangeable lift ticket. Summit County resorts all offer topflight skiing and golf, some of the West's best outlet shopping and a myriad of special winter events, summer festivals and other sports opportunities.

Winter Park, also less than two hours from Denver, is the only resort in the Rockies with direct ski-train service. Its wide-ranging terrain has long been a favorite with budget-conscious Denver skiers and vacationers. With no definable town center, Winter Park has long offered

Did You Know. . .

. . . that the *average* price of a home in high-toned Aspen and Snowmass is over a million dollars? The median price is somewhere in the stratosphere.

first-rate skiing with scattered resort amenities. Now, after years of planning and negotiating with the U.S. Forest Service and other agencies, Winter Park is poised to develop a village at the base of the lifts.

Nearby SilverCreek, one of the country's best learn-to-ski areas, sits entirely on private land and never had problems building. However, the financially troubled little resort long bristled with For Sale signs. It was purchased by Brazilian investors in August 1995, and in the following six months, building lots appreciated by about $10,000 each and home resales did too.

Steamboat, in northern Colorado, is acknowledged as one of the state's preeminent "powder pockets." In January 1996, for instance, the resort was blessed with more than 220 inches of snow. Lodging choices abound both in the ranch town-turned-resort town of Steamboat Springs and built-for-skiing Steamboat. The ski terrain drapes seductively over three peaks on one mountain massif—with lifts and runs soon slated for a fourth.

Telluride, tucked into a deep valley in southwestern Colorado, is, like Aspen, a Victorian gem that was a down-at-the-heels mining town until skiing took hold. It long had a reputation for steep and uncrowded slopes, deep snow and an irreverent counterculture scene with summer festivals that included film, mushrooms, bluegrass, and jazz to fill in the slack months. The '90s put a new spin on old Telluride. A Beaver Creek-style resort called Telluride Mountain Village took shape, boasting a first-rate golf course, a mammoth hotel, seven-figure-priced homes (one belongs to Oprah Winfrey), and six-figure-priced condominiums.

The Rest of the Rockies . . .

Utah's license plate slogan reads "The Greatest Snow on Earth," a boast on wheels about the best powder skiing in the country where ski-resort development is severely concentrated. In fact, the state's only true ski resort is Park City, once a mining town and now the center-

A Word of Caution

If you're thinking of purchasing land and building your own mountain retreat, be aware that long-time residents in some mountain communities and mountain states feel threatened by the influx of leisure-home owners and even by newcomers buying year-round residences. Many locals feel they are being priced out of the real estate market as they see ranch and farmland being gobbled up for golf courses and housing subdivisions, valleys becoming choked with residential development and the traffic it brings, open space surrounding existing towns diminishing, and threats to the wilderness. In fact, many locals believe that an entire way of life is under siege.

Local residents' response may be lengthy and costly approval processes for new development, caps on annual building construction in a community, and even creative taxation. Colorado's Pitkin County (home to Aspen and Snowmass), for instance, has adopted "Rural and Remote" zoning to protect isolated mountain parcels from overdevelopment. To balance the economic hardship that could stem from restrictions on private property (and therefore potential sales of land to someone who might build an excessively large home on it), development rights are being transferred for use elsewhere. The *Aspen Times* reported that Gerald Hines, who has proposed a new luxury-home subdivision at the base of Aspen Highlands, was opening negotiations with backcountry land owners for $150,000 per development right.

At this writing, Vermont was tweaking a property tax proposal that would impose a statewide school tax on all new second-home construction. The Colorado legislature has been kicking around the notion of a county-option real estate transfer tax on unincorporated land (i.e., land under county jurisdiction beyond city or town boundaries).

piece for phenomenal skiing. Park City has three ski areas—four counting Utah Winter Sports Park, the new ski-jumping and bobsled venue for the 2002 Winter Olympics. Park City is close enough to booming Salt Lake City for permanent residents to commute from there although Park City maintains its resort ambiance.

The Park City Ski Area is Utah's giant ski area and is the headquarters for the U.S. ski team. It offers direct lift access from town and from a new commercial and condo development called the Resort Center. There you have a choice of recreational racing, night skiing, bowl skiing and wonderful cruising terrain. Deer Valley is part of Park City and an ultraluxurious resort unto itself. Wolf Mountain, the third and scrappiest of Park City's ski areas, is Deer Valley's polar opposite. The only one of the trio to permit snowboarding, it exudes youthful energy. Other sizable Utah ski areas—Alta, Brighton, Powder Mountain, Snowbasin, Snowbird, Solitude and Sundance—offer abundant terrain, frequent accumulations of knee-deep powder and spectacular Wasatch scenery.

Parts of New Mexico are true Sun Belt and desert locales, but Sangre de Cristo Range in the north is true Rocky Mountains. Taos Ski Valley is a western classic. This vest-pocket ski resort nestles into a tiny valley at the base of some of the country's most interesting and challenging ski slopes. Taos's Ernie Blake Ski School is frequently cited as the best in the country, and it certainly is one where even good skiers enroll to become better still. The resort packs a two-for-one wallop. You'll find ample additional lodging, a temperate year-round climate, and fine dining and fine art in the town of Taos on a high desert plateau 18 miles from the ski resort.

Other nearby resorts offer low-key skiing and excellent values: the funky, laid-back town of Red River and its namesake ski area; the Angel Fire resort with on-site skiing, golf and vacation homes; and Ski Rio with its wide-ranging ski terrain and a nascent resort development. These have long been secret spots for budget-conscious skiers from Texas and Oklahoma.

Wyoming skiing is virtually synonymous with Jackson Hole, a huge, rough-and-ready mountain about an hour's drive from the southern entrance to Yellowstone National Park. Its relentlessly steep slopes have given it a reputation for merciless challenge that draws some of the best skiers in the country, but it has a tamer side too. Here you'll find outstanding cross-country skiing, snowmobile tours to Yellowstone, and the legitimate Old West town of Jackson without its hordes of summer tourists, who come to visit the town's two neighboring national parks, Yellowstone and Teton, and the bustling town itself with its good shops, restaurants and varied diversions.

In addition to justifiably famous Jackson Hole, nearby Grand Targhee is a beguiling ski destination, developed by its architect-owner to provide both a congenial resort setting and outstanding snow conditions. Jackson Hole, Grand Targhee and a smaller area in the town of Jackson called Snow King market a joint lift ticket.

Sun Valley is the monarch of Idaho. Skiing came to a former sheep pasture in the shadow of the Sawtooth Mountains back in 1936, when the world's first chairlift was erected there. Once a glamorous retreat for such Hollywood stars as Norma Shearer, Claudette Colbert and Errol Flynn, it has remained one of North America's major ski mountains for some six decades. The main ski area is on giant Bald Mountain, which boasts some of the best cruising trails, bowls and mogul runs in the country. If you want to learn how to ski, you can't do better than Dollar Mountain, one of the world's preeminent beginner ski areas. And if you love to skate, do some laps on the outdoor rink where famous skaters from Sonja Henie to Katarina Witt have performed.

Outstanding cross-country skiing is among other winter activities, and golf, fly fishing and hiking are the big summer diversions. Sun Valley's neighboring town of Ketchum is the place the Hemingway family calls home (grandpa Ernest wrote *For Whom the Bell Tolls* there). Bruce Willis and Demi Moore are today's best-known celebrities. Willis, in fact, is so taken with the region that he has bought much of downtown Ketchum, including a historic theater.

Idaho's other ski resorts are scattered throughout this huge, L-shaped state. Brundage Mountain near McCall is a laid-back charmer near Payette Lake north of Boise. You'll find two growing resorts in the Panhandle with better access from Spokane than Boise.

Schweitzer Mountain, just 11 miles north of the lakeside town of Sandpoint, is the state's northernmost ski area. It combines sweeping terrain, topside views of Lake Pend Oreille and a compact little resort development. The 43-mile-long lake boasts a summer's worth of terrific sailing, windsurfing, water skiing and motorboating. Golf, hiking, tennis and special summer festivals also abound.

Montana is a big state, and its two leading ski resorts are big, both in name and in scale. The Big Mountain is in northwestern Montana, near (by Montana standards) Glacier National Park and Flathead Lake. Big Sky is in southwestern Montana near Yellowstone National Park and Ted Turner and Jane Fonda's 107,000-acre Flying D Ranch.

The Big Mountain is one of the continent's rare ski areas that offers skiing on all sides of a high peak whose summit flirts with the timberline and whose lower runs are carved through a dense forest. Accommodations are available in a growing master-planned development at the base of the mountain or in the lakeside resort town of Whitefish, which is known for phenomenal water sports and even better golf.

Aptly named Big Sky stretches from a golf-oriented lower section to a ski-oriented upper one. An aggressive expansion program begun during the summer of 1996 includes a village center. The icing on the cake of Big Sky's totally sublime skiing is a sky-scraping tram, which debuted during the 1995–96 ski season to access the awesomely steep slopes of Lone Peak. The result is a great variety of terrain. Summer visitors pepper the golf course, flock to Yellowstone, whose western entrance is less than an hour's drive away, and fly fish in the nearby Gallatin River, the aquatic star of *A River Runs Through It*.

. . . And Elsewhere in the West

The Sierra Nevada forms a natural barrier between California and Nevada. In this rugged range, you'll find Yosemite, Sequoia and Kings Canyon National Parks as well as Lake Tahoe, which San Francisco Bay Area skiers have long viewed as their private playground. This huge, improbably blue lake, so deep that it never freezes, is a scenic wonder in its own right.

Tahoe shines particularly in winter with legendary snow accumulations and North America's largest concentration of ski areas—ten downhill and seven cross-country. Heavenly Resort and Sierra-at-Tahoe on the South Shore and Squaw Valley USA, Alpine Meadows and Northstar-at-Tahoe are the largest Alpine areas, and the North Shore's Royal Gorge boasts the most extensive trail system of any Nordic area in the land.

Tahoe actually draws more people in summer, a good argument for visiting in winter, but there's no arguing with the quality golf, hiking in the nearby Desolation Wilderness, and boating and other water sports. Reno is the gateway, while South Lake Tahoe, Tahoe City, Donner Lake, Truckee and Incline Village are the major accommodation centers.

A popular spot for Angeleños escaping the southern California heat is Mammoth Lakes. Mammoth Mountain is a West Coast giant with more than 3,100 vertical feet of skiing, ranging from the most gut-grabbing headwalls to the mildest of beginner slopes. Snowfalls can be so prodigious that the ski season usually kicks off in November and sometimes lasts until the Fourth of July. Along with its nearby sister resort of June Mountain, Mammoth Mountain offers the biggest and the best skiing within reasonable weekend distance of Los Angeles. In summer, golf, hiking, mountain biking, scenic lift rides, shopping and water sports are the appeals. The Big Bear Lake area requires one-third the driving time from L.A., the major tradeoff being midsize rather than mammoth ski mountains. Snow Summit and Bear Mountain check in with verticals of 1,200 and 1,665 respectively and a greater reliance on snowmaking than the Tahoe areas to the north.

The town of Bend, Oregon, has developed one of America's capitals of the sporty lifestyle. Skiing at nearby Mt. Bachelor, hiking, outstanding golf, topnotch biking, rock climbing and other active pursuits keep vacationers busy around the calendar—literally, because the golfing and biking season overlaps with skiing. Mt. Bachelor averages 25 feet of snow a year and normally is able to run lifts from November until July. In fact, when you read a newspaper report with a Bend dateline about the U.S. Ski Team's summer training camps, which are to ski racing what spring training is to baseball, it's really happening at Mt. Bachelor.

THE EAST

Three New England states within weekend driving distance of some of the nation's most populous metropolitan areas boast the lion's share of resorts in the East. If the image is of old-fashioned white farmhouses, red barns and syrup buckets hanging from maples, the reality is growing slopeside developments, state-of-the-art ski lifts, snowmaking and an increasingly sophisticated resort scene.

Vermont is top of the heap. Its southernmost ski area is Mt. Snow, which has incorporated adjacent Carinthia and nearby Haystack into one megadestination. Mt. Snow's wide runs, four-hour drive from the New York area and excellent summer programs, including golf and mountain biking, make it perennially popular. Stratton has similar characteristics but is a little further from New York and a lot closer to the big shopping outlets around Manchester.

Killington is the East's largest ski area with skiing on 162 trails and slopes draped over six interlinked peaks and accessed by 20 lifts (including the country's longest, fanciest gondola) and blanketed with snow from a behemoth snowmaking system. It also boasts the East's longest ski season, with small-scale operations normally beginning in October and winding down in early June. An 18-hole championship golf course, noteworthy tennis school, hiking, mountain biking, fly fishing and organized family adventures make Killington a top summer vacation spot too. Okemo is a central Vermont neighbor with big-time size, scale and facilities, while Ascutney is a small, family-oriented resort.

Northern Vermont's giants are Sugarbush and Stowe. Sugarbush is now the closest rival to Killington in terms of size. With a lift connecting two previously separate ski areas, Sugarbush is now one megamountain with six interconnected peaks, 18 lifts, and 111 trails. Sugarbush skiers have a huge choice of accommodations and dining, and in summer the options extend to an 18-hole Robert Trent Jones, Sr., golf course; 35 tennis courts, horseback riding, hiking and other sports.

Stowe remains the self-styled "ski capital of the East," combining great skiing on two nearby mountain complexes, an atmospheric town and a strip of restaurants, shops and lodgings along the Mountain Road that is hard to beat. Stowe has a long history of downhill skiing, but it was also one of the pioneering eastern resorts to develop extensive cross-country skiing. Stowe's accommodations include slopeside condominiums, luxurious homes, achingly charming bed-and-breakfast inns, budget motels and even timeshares called the Trapp Family Guesthouses. Yes, those Trapps—of *Sound of Music* fame. Bolton Valley, Jay Peak, Smugglers' Notch and Northern Star (formerly Burke Mountain) comprise a quartet of smaller, more economical family-friendly resorts in Vermont's north country.

New Hampshire's prime ski resorts are concentrated in two regions: along Interstate 93 and in the Mt. Washington Valley. (Kancamagus Highway is a very scenic east-west route connecting them.) Loon Mountain and Waterville Valley are the largest and most diverse of the "Ski 93" resorts, while Attitash/Bear Peak and Cranmore lead the Mt. Washington Valley pack. A midweek vacation lift ticket is valid at more than a dozen New Hampshire mountains, enabling you to sample them all (and accompanying children to even ski free). North Conway, the largest town in Mt. Washington Valley, has become one of the Northeast's most popular meccas of shopping outlets. Maine's main resorts are Sugarloaf and Sunday, two giants with exceptional terrain and growing resort developments.

CANADA

Because of the relative weakness of the Canadian dollar, Canada is an economical choice for a ski vacation—and, in some locales, a ski vacation home. Your choices are the mountainous portions of British Columbia and Alberta in western Canada and Quebec in the east.

Number one in Canada—and by many measures number one in North America—is Whistler Village in British Columbia's Coast Range. This exquisitely planned vacation village nestles at the foot of Whistler and Blackcomb mountains, North America's largest ski mountains. Summer activities include golf on three championship courses, tennis, sailing on Alta Lake, trails for hiking and mountain horseback riding, and countless other diversions.

British Columbia's interior Okanagan Valley—a wine-growing region often compared to California's Napa or Sonoma counties—is a significant golf destination and is increasingly known for its skiing. Wild West–style Silver Star, with cheerful Victorian-hued buildings; Big White, which launched a contemporary classic development in 1996; and Apex Alpine are major ski mountains poised for the big time. Sun Peaks, a huge ski area formerly called Tod Mountain, is remaking itself into a major ski and golf resort with a new base village.

Four contiguous national parks form the spine of Canada along the British Columbia–Alberta border. Banff, Jasper, Yoho and Kootenay parks are unsurpassed in their splendid natural beauty. In and around these parks, you'll find outstanding skiing and bustling towns. Banff is the best place to stay to sample skiing at three nearby ski areas (Lake Louise, Sunshine and Norquay) and offers excellent lodging, shopping, dining and nightlife. Jasper is a mini-Banff, with one nearby ski area (Marmot Basin) and ancillary resort facilities and services.

Tremblant is eastern Canada's rising superstar ski area. Both Tremblant, located 80 miles from Montreal, and Mont Ste.-Anne, just 25 miles from Québec City, offer first-rate skiing, nearby lodging and a delightful French ambiance. Skiing here feels like going to Europe without crossing an ocean.

FOR MORE INFORMATION

All the major ski magazines—*Skiing, Ski* and *Powder*—report extensively about skiing and ski resorts. But *Snow Country* is so committed to the mountain lifestyle that it also publishes a regular column on real estate in ski towns and covers mountain lifestyles extensively. An annual subscription is $15.97. The subscription address is *Snow Country,* PO Box 2071, Harlan, IA 51593-2270.

KEEP IN MIND

➤ Ski resorts are exceptionally well set up for their heavy seasonal business, which peaks between Thanksgiving and Easter.

➤ Most ski resorts have central reservation services, which package many components of a ski trip. They also make it easy to rent a place to stay—or to rent out *your* place to other vacationers once you've purchased.

➤ Since summer is off-season in ski towns, that's the time to snag the best vacation values.

CHAPTER 12

Enjoying the Idyllic Islands

Ah, the images were inspired by *Robinson Crusoe* . . . or perhaps *Fantasy Island.* Few of us can resist the thought of escaping to a palm-studded paradise surrounded by warm seas and caressed by balmy breezes. From Barbados to the Big Island of Hawaii, sun-kissed map dots rising from Caribbean and Pacific waters are the stuff of dreams. Having an island condo or village to call home evokes sublime beaches for relaxing along with golfing, swimming, snorkeling, scuba diving, sailing, surfing, windsurfing and sport fishing. In many cases, fine (or at least interesting) restaurants, great nightlife and fantastic shopping fill the best tropical resorts under the sun. Many spots even offer aesthetic stimulation: arts and crafts, museums, historical sites. In this age of ecotourism and adventure travel, wildlife sanctuaries and opportunities for hiking and biking are important to many vacationers who are thinking of putting down roots.

HAWAII

On December 7, 1941, the Japanese bombing of Pearl Harbor catapulted the United States into World War II and a paradisiacal group of Pacific islands into the history books and the nation's collective conscience. Less than 16 years later, the islands became the fiftieth state.

Top Ten Islands

In 1996, *Condé Nast Traveler* added an island category to its Reader's Choice Awards. The winners, based on its sophisticated readers' evaluations of each island's environment/scenery, accommodations, activities, and people, were:

1. Maui (Hawaii)

2. Kauai (Hawaii)

3. Bermuda

4. The Big Island (Hawaii)

5. Bali (Indonesia)

6. Vancouver Island (British Columbia)

7. Cape Breton Island (Nova Scotia)

8. Bora Bora and Moorea (tie)

10. Phuket (Thailand)

Honolulu, the state capital and number-one city, is where it all happened. Located on a gorgeous natural bay on the south side of the island of Oahu, it was the site of the attack. Pearl Harbor is just a portion of the bay, and the city that has grown up by the sea and on the hillsides is now also a mid-Pacific hub. Skyscraper office towers, the University of Hawaii, enormous shopping centers and the condominium high-rises of Waikiki Beach produce a distinct urban atmosphere. Oahu is more than just Honolulu, of course, so if you like the convenient airport but prefer a tropical escape that doesn't feature traffic lights or parking meters, consider exploring the other coasts—or other islands.

Did You Know...

... that Waialeale on Kauai is the wettest place in the United States with an annual average of 444 inches of rain?

Kauai is the only major island located northwest of Oahu. Typhoon Iniki in September 1992 devastated much of it, but recovery has been fast and thorough. Known as the Garden Island, Kauai is a fascinating and romantic place. Lihue, an old plantation settlement, is the only community that could be called a city. The first Hawaiian island on which Captain Cook set foot was Kauai, and the place where he first stepped is now the town of Waimea. Today it is the jumping-off point for breathtaking Waimea Canyon, which is ten miles long, half-a-mile deep and more than a mile wide. Other natural spectacles include Alakai Swamp, Kaana Ridge and the view down to the lush Kalalu Valley.

Did You Know. . .

. . . that Hawaii is America's most ethnically diverse state and one of the most multicultural of all island groups? According to the 1990 census, 61.8 percent of the inhabitants identified themselves as Asians or Pacific Islanders, 33.4 as Caucasian, 7.3 percent as Hispanic, and 2.5 percent as African-Americans. In truth, many Hawaiians are racially mixed.

Molokai and nearby Lanai are set in a brilliant sea to the southeast of Oahu and are its closest neighbors. Molokai is a sparsely populated place that styles itself as the Friendly Island. It was not always so, for it was originally Hawaii's leper colony. Lanai, a gem of an island, is noteworthy for its pineapple fields, fine beachcombing and exceptional scuba diving and snorkeling even by Hawaiian standards. Development has begun, but both islands will most likely remain more low-key and controlled than their neighbors.

The next island down the chain is Maui, famous as a surfer's paradise. It also boasts such top-ranked golf-oriented resorts as Kaanapali, Kapalua Bay and Wailea, and more than 80 sand beaches of many hues, including glowing gold, lava black and even a rare red. Dominating the northwestern portion of the island, Kaanapali was Hawaii's first major built-for-leisure resort development. Wailea followed with a particular emphasis on golf. This resort on the southwestern shore features three championship courses and two clubhouses. The charming old whaling town of Lahaina on Maui's central west shore has developed a reputation as something of an art colony. Inland is Haleakala, a

Air Today. Gone Tomorrow?

If you're thinking of purchasing Hawaiian property for your own use as well as for renting, you need to think about the islands' accessibility. According to the Hawaii Visitors Bureau, seats on scheduled (i.e., noncharter) airlines have been eroding from their 1990 peak, which may mean that the frequent-flyer allotment many people plan to use for vacationing has been down significantly for most airlines. The picture may turn around, however. United Airlines, the major carrier, announced plans to increase seats from the mainland and Japan by 12.4 percent for the summer of 1996.

Year	Seats	Change
1990	7,367,310	—
1991	7,157,210	- 2.6%
1992	6,362,440	-11.1
1993	5,882,460	- 7.5
1994	5,551,870	- 5.6
1995 (Jan.-May)*	2,300,000	- 2.3

Travelers arriving on the Hawaiian islands came from the following places during the first 11 months of 1995:

U.S. Mainland	2,999,380	- 0.1% from 1994
Asia/Pacific	2,400,210	+ 9.0
Europe/Other	440,220	+ 0.5
Canada	211,610	- 4.0

These numbers may change significantly when Japan Airlines' new thrice-weekly nonstops between Tokyo and the Big Island, inaugurated in July 1996, are factored into the equation.

*1994 figures are the latest full-year statistics available at this writing; after the first five months of 1995, which showed a further 1.2 percent decline, the bureau stopped gathering these figures.

10,000-foot, dormant volcano whose summit, accessible by car, affords breathtaking views of this enchanted island. Arriving before dawn and watching the sun rise from the top is one of the more memorable travel experiences you can have.

Top Scuba Sites

The readers of *Rodale's Scuba Diving* ranked the top five Caribbean/Atlantic scuba diving spots as follows:

1. Little Cayman, Cayman Islands

2. San Salvador, Bahamas

3. Cayman Brac, Cayman Islands and Puerto Rico (tie)

5. Bonaire

The Big Island—Hawaii—is Hawaii's giant. This fascinating place has relatively few standard beaches (those that exist tend to be of the black-sand variety), but it boasts an unsurpassed abundance of nature's wonders. Its land area exceeds that of all the other islands combined. Much of its mass is the product of Mauna Kea's epic volcanic eruptions. Cresting at 13,796 feet above the level of the very nearby sea, Mauna Kea not only is Hawaii's loftiest point but, because it rises directly from the ocean floor, is actually the world's tallest mountain. When measured from its sea-floor base to its summit, it is higher than Mt. Everest.

The Big Island is in transition from the standpoint of development and topographically. It currently has the world's most aggressive volcano action, which you can see as close as the rangers permit. Volcanoes National Park boasts a wondrous display of ongoing eruptions, lava flows and hissing steam vents. Hilo is the Big Island's largest city and commercial hub, but Kailua-Kona, one of Hawaii's oldest towns, is more interesting. It is awash with history and has etched itself into America's sports consciousness as the site of the famous Ironman Triathlon.

As the farthest island from Oahu and the most "local," large-scale leisure development came late to the Big Island. First came the luxury hotels, with second-home communities following more recently. The highlands with their coffee plantations (that's where Kona coffee is grown) and the inland valley of Waimea, noteworthy as a rich ranch-land with a unique tropical cowboy culture, have always had their fans and are interesting for visitors or anyone wishing a hideaway in a traditional Hawaiian community.

All-Island Festival

For six weeks each fall, Aloha Festivals on each island honor the tradition of *makahiki*, a festival of music, dance and feasting. Since *makahiki* originally meant that war was not permitted, it was deemed a suitable tradition to celebrate the end of World War II. The first Aloha Festival took place in 1946, and now it has grown to a major Pacific event attended by upwards of a million people. Highlights are the Aloha Festival Flower Parade and other events on Oahu in mid-September along with events on Kauai, the Big Island, Maui, Lanai and Molokai through the third week in October. For festival information, call 800-852-7690, 808-944-8857.

THE CARIBBEAN

The West Indies comprise hundreds of islands in a vast arc stretching from just off the Florida coast to Venezuela. Ranging from volcanic cones to little outcroppings that barely break the surface of the sea, they present a vast choice of terrain, vegetation and style. They include heavily populated, vibrant cities as well as true hideaways, and the islands' cultural mix matches their geographical diversity. The roots of many islands tap deep into Amerindian, African, Spanish, French and English culture, and some have Dutch or East Indian influences as well. With a highly developed resort scene and tourist orientation, the West Indies offer visitors much to do—or nothing at all. Tourism has supplanted agriculture and fishing as the chief economic factor throughout the Caribbean, and with tourism come many opportunities to buy your own piece of an island paradise.

The Bahamas

Though technically not in the Caribbean, the Bahamas *feel* Caribbean. Sprinkled across 100,000 square miles of Atlantic Ocean are 700 islands, but only twenty are considered populated. They share so much history with their true Caribbean neighbors that we tend to think of them the same way. Some, like Bimini and Grand Bahama, are just a few miles offshore from South Florida, while those at the southeastern end of the archipelago are distant and remote. Like parts of Florida, the Bahamas' climate is a product of the Gulf Stream and trade winds, which bring hot summers and benign winters. The Bahamas have more annual variation in weather than other islands.

Did You Know. . .

. . . that one of the Bahamas, Eleuthera, along the edge of the Grand Bahama Bank, is 100 miles long but less than 3 miles wide?

Nassau on Grand Providence Island (the Bahamian capital) and Freeport on Grand Bahama are the biggest cities. They attract the most visitors, as cruise ship passengers and short-hop flyers from Florida come over for brief spurts of shopping and gambling. Paradise Island, connected to Nassau by causeway, is a good choice if you like a well-developed resort near a significant city. Montrejau, a 13th century Augustinian cloister, is the oldest building in the Bahamas and the oldest European structure in the Western Hemisphere. It was dismantled in France and rebuilt in Versailles Gardens on Paradise Island in 1962. That was just about the time that Freeport and nearby Lucaya were being developed as a major tourist center. The town of West End is just 55 miles from Florida, which makes Grand Bahama the most accessible island to the U.S. mainland. It offers a well-developed tourist infrastructure, good shopping, nightlife, golf, tennis and scuba diving.

Taken as a whole, the island nation is not really about big cities. Smaller islands fringed with soft-sand beaches floating in a warm, shallow sea and intimate, picturesque villages are so appealing that you never want to leave. Some islands are rural and remote; others, like Eleuthera, have enough modern trappings and luxury to please the most particular travelers.

FAMILY ISLANDS

Everywhere but major destinations are lumped into the category of family islands, and these appeal to anyone seeking a quieter retreat. Nicknamed "the top of the Bahamas," the Abacos are an anomaly. While most Bahamians are the black descendants of former African slaves, the Abacos' earliest settlers were white loyalists who fled after the American Revolution, adding a bit of New England to the Abaconian lifestyle on this island cluster just east of Grand Bahama.

Treasure Island is the new promotional name for Great Guana, which was rechristened with the development and burgeoning of cruise ships. Other islands retain their quiet charm. The largest is Andros, just west of Grand Bahama. Its scuba diving and snorkeling on the world's third-longest barrier reef are world-class and birdwatching is just as good. Andros also offers excellent bonefishing. Bimini Islands, the setting for Ernest Hemingway's *Islands in the Stream,* with their soft, tan sand beaches offer tranquility and more outstanding bonefishing. Other islands—the Berrys, Cat, the Exumas, for example—are secluded getaways for relaxing, swimming, snorkeling, birding and other quiet pursuits.

The Greater Antilles

Cuba, Jamaica, Hispaniola and Puerto Rico are the four largest Caribbean islands; and other than the Bahamas, they are also the ones closest to Florida. In addition, they are the most vibrant islands—the ones that make the most headlines, boast the greatest variety of attractions and appeal to the most adventuresome travelers.

Puerto Rico.   The easiest of the fabulous foursome to reach is Puerto Rico, a commonwealth affiliated with the United States whose residents are American citizens. Located 1,000 miles from Miami, it has both Atlantic and Caribbean coasts. It is also the smallest and most easterly of the Greater Antilles. With shockingly good air service from the East Coast or from anywhere via Miami, it is promoting itself as "the Continent of Puerto Rico." This marketing message clearly conveys the ambiance of a foreign country while remaining in the red, white and blue orbit. Prosperous and stable, it mingles Hispanic sauciness with mainland economics—and makes it work.

Like many of its Caribbean neighbors, Puerto Rico is a mountainous island fringed with palm-studded beaches—in this case, 300 miles of white sand. The capital, San Juan, is a genuine big city with a modern beat. With its office buildings, casinos and busy port, it looks, acts, and feels modern, but the city's soul remains in the picturesque historic center of Old San Juan. Don't miss the stunning Spanish fortress called El Morro, which guarded the harbor from the sixteenth century through the early years of the twentieth.

San Juan is to Puerto Rico what Miami is to Florida. Each is an urban giant that energizes an entire region. Once you get out of the bustling metropolitan area, you see the rest of Puerto Rico in a different, calmer light. With 15 manicured golf courses, Puerto Rico has been described as "Scotland with sun." Beyond the fairways, the island offers great natural beauty too. Luquillo Beach and El Yunque, a 28,000-acre rain forest, are both close enough to San Juan for a short excursion. The lively little cities of Mayagüez on the west coast and Ponce on the south coast demand more time. These more relaxed centers are worthy of consideration as leisure property.

Did You Know. . .

. . . that over 2.5 million people live in Puerto Rico, while some 2.7 million Puerto Ricans reside on the U.S. mainland?

Hispaniola.   Hispaniola, which is west of Puerto Rico, east of Cuba and northeast of Jamaica, is the Caribbean's second-largest island after Cuba. The Dominican Republic and Haiti share the island, and each has a different but equally checkered history filled with intrigues, dictators and revolutions spanning the centuries. Yet both are fascinating and appeal to adventurous travelers (and adventurous leisure-home buyers).

The Dominican Republic is very Spanish in flavor and in language, whereas Haiti, whose languages are French and a Creole *patois*, feels very African. With soaring mountains (including 10,416-foot Pico Duarte, the Caribbean's highest peak), dense forests, abundant wildlife and beaches that can still be called undiscovered, the Dominican Republic is rich in natural beauty. Tourist developments are mushrooming but, once you get away from bursting-at-the-seams Santo Domingo, you still feel you're on a "real" island rather than a tourist's one.

Jamaica.   The third-largest island is Jamaica. Tucked under the wings of eastern Cuba and western Hispaniola, it is an enduringly popular vacation spot. Stunning beaches, heavily treed hillsides and outstanding tourist facilities lure visitors. Yet the birthplace of reggae marches to its own beat. Kingston, Jamaica's sprawling capital on the south coast, houses over a million inhabitants, while Montego Bay and Negril in western Jamaica and Ocho Rios on the northeastern coast are the best-known resorts and most developed areas. Port Antonio on the northeastern shore is a mellow harbor town where Errol Flynn lived; Mandeville is a quiet community and the center of Jamaica's coffee industry. The beguiling Blue Mountain highlands and cascading waterfalls are popular inland excursions.

Cuba.   Since Fidel Castro took the reins of power in Cuba nearly 40 years ago, this huge and vibrant island nation has essentially been off-limits to Americans, but investors and tourists from other nations have no such prohibitions. Cuba's appeal includes low prices, an enthusiastic welcome for tourists and their spending power, and a growing array of modern, internationally oriented resorts in an island nation that otherwise seems like a place time forgot. Despite being just 90 miles from the Florida Keys, at this writing Cuba remains a European and Canadian destination, but time and politics do change, so it's a place to keep an eye on.

The Cayman Islands.   The Cayman Islands, a trio of low-slung coral outcroppings, barely rise from sparkling Caribbean waters. They aren't big enough to be counted among the Greater Antilles, but with their location some 180 miles west of Jamaica, there's no other geographical grouping in which they could fit. The Caymans have become noteworthy as a tax-free haven (including property tax) with unrestricted foreign ownership of property and banking laws that have earned the nickname "Switzerland of the Caribbean."

Vacationers, however, often care less about international finance and more about the Caymans' exceptional scuba diving. Grand Cayman wraps around a generous bay called North Island. A narrow peninsula resembling a mirror image of Cape Cod comprises the western portion of the island, with most of the island's resorts lined up along Seven Mile Beach on the west coast and bustling capital of George Town at the base. Divers and snorkelers make pilgrimages to Sting Ray City to mingle with huge stingrays that have become so used to humans that they are practically tame. They live in a sandbar-protected shallow, just 12 feet deep. Little Cayman and Cayman Brac, respectively 75 and 90 miles offshore, are laid-back nature lovers' delights. Diving, diving, more diving, snorkeling, birdwatching, caving and bonefishing are the main diversions on all three islands.

The Lesser Antilles

This wide-ranging archipelago curves in a huge arc from the Virgin Islands just east of Puerto Rico. The largest islands, St. Croix and St. Thomas, plus St. John just offshore from St. Thomas, are U.S. possessions, while Tortola, Virgin Gorda and several smaller islands comprise the British Virgins. Hilly landscapes, breeze-kissed highlands, shimmering beaches, excellent waters for sailing, deep-sea fishing and scuba diving, and some of the Caribbean's best towns characterize these enchanted islands. Power shoppers are drawn to the U.S. Virgins because of their duty-free status, enabling each traveler to bring up to $1,200 in custom-free goods back to the mainland. Although it was badly battered in the 1995 hurricane season, St. Thomas's main town of Charlotte Amalie remains the number-one cruise port in the Caribbean, and many passengers are so enchanted that they take their next island vacation there.

Did You Know. . .

. . . that Anguilla, one of the Leeward Islands and a largely self-governing jurisdiction that is nevertheless one of five remaining British Dependent Territories, has done away with business taxes in order to establish itself as an offshore financial center? Anguilla therefore collects no income, capital gains, estate, profit or other direct taxes.

The Leeward Islands are among the Caribbean's most tranquil hideaways. English-speaking, but with a beguiling Caribbean lilt, many of these islands were sighted by Columbus on one or another of his voyages and were shuttled by war and/or treaty between Spain, France, Holland and England. Today they offer sailing, sun, sand and sea in lavish disproportion to their modest size. The islands curve southeastward from the Virgins in two distinct bands. The inner or western group is comprised of Saba, St. Eustatius, St. Kitts, Nevis, and Montserrat. The outer or eastern group includes Anguilla, St. Martin and St. Barts in one cluster, and Antigua and Barbuda in another.

Did You Know. . .

. . . that, at 37 square miles, St. Martin/Sint Maarten is the smallest island in the world to be under the jurisdiction of two separate sovereign nations?

Windward Islands

Guadeloupe is located at the eastern apex of the Lesser Antilles arc, and the roughly parallel lines of two islands merge into one. Some call Guadeloupe the southernmost Leeward and some the northernmost Windward. In either case, Guadeloupe and nearby Martinique are full-fledged overseas *départements* of France. Dominica, between them, is an independent country of English derivation. They are three of the larger islands and among the most brilliant jewels. Volcanic summits that catch the clouds, beaches of exceptional beauty even by Caribbean standards, nature preserves, rich historic legacies and cultural distinctions make them worth a long look.

St. Lucia, whose emblem is twin volcanic cones known as the Pitons, rises majestically from the blue waters just south of Martinique. These peaks are fitting symbols of the pride the island has exhibited since gaining its independence in 1979. It has mushroomed from a sleepy hideaway into a booming tourist island with golf courses, beach resorts, a major port for cruise ships and an unabashed ambition to be a top holiday destination. Immediately to the south are the Grenadines, also known as the Nutmeg Islands, which are smaller, equally gorgeous and much more sanguine. St. Vincent, Grenada, Bequia, Carriocou, Petit Martinique, Petty St. Vincent and other, even smaller islands are perfect for sailing, scuba diving, snorkeling, swimming, sunning and otherwise getting away from whatever you wish to escape.

Barbados sits far out in the ocean, roughly east of St. Vincent. Of all the islands, it is the most English, going so far as to have erected a statue of Lord Nelson in Trafalgar Square. Towns have names like

Christ Church, St. Michael, St. Peter, St. James, St. Andrew and Bridge-town. Police officers are called bobbies (and they wear those tall English helmets even in the tropical sun), and cricket is the national sport.

Coastal Islands

Just off the Venezuelan coast are more distinctive islands. Trinidad and Tobago comprise one country with two cultures. Trinidad, just eight miles offshore, is a large, urban, rather industrialized and multi-cultural island (African, Amerindian, East Indian, European, Middle Eastern, Chinese). It is where the steel drum—now the all-purpose Caribbean instrument—was invented and where a pre-Lenten Carnival that is the peer of New Orleans' or Rio de Janeiro's takes place. Tobago is much smaller and infinitely more rural. It is one of several islands that claims to have been the model for the *Robinson Crusoe* tale.

Margarita Island has long been an escape valve for vacationers from Caracas and other busy South American cities. It traces its history to pre-Columbian pearl gatherers. The Spanish colonized it, and in contrast to other islands that changed hands many times, Isla de Margarita has remained Spanish. Porlomar and Pampatar on the southeast corner of this 8-by-40-mile island are the main tourist centers, with great sand beaches (the longest measures 18 miles and is a lot bigger than some Caribbean islands), oodles of hotels and holiday apartments, and lots of shops.

Though independent, the fabled ABC islands (Aruba, Bonaire and Curaçao) are still often called the Dutch West Indies (or Netherlands Antilles). These low-slung, arid islands possess a particularly benign climate with steady, year-round temperatures and very little rain. Aruba is the Dutch West Indies' mighty midget. Though the smallest of the trio, it developed its tourist infrastructure first and most. The quaint capital of Oranjestad, the ruins of a castle built in 1499 and fabulous beaches and massive casino-hotels make this a top destination that appeals to vacationers of all tastes. To prevent the island from being overdeveloped, the government is in the process of transforming one-fourth of it into a national park. For economic reasons, redevelopment efforts are being encouraged around San Nicolas, a former refinery area on the tip of the island.

Curaçao, the largest and most built-up of the three, also retains the most unrefined Dutch atmosphere. Ornate rowhouses that would be at home in Amsterdam, but with vibrant tropical paint jobs, make the

Hurricanes

When a hurricane sweeps across the sea and strikes land on a small and vulnerable map speck, it makes headlines. There is always property damage and sometimes loss of life, but once cleanup is over, tourism appears to rebound and is often strengthened in the wake of a storm. In 1989, for instance, no island was harder hit by Hurricane Hugo than St. Croix in the U.S. Virgin Islands. Six years later, during the awesome 1995 storm season, St. Croix remained unscathed as Hurricane Marilyn battered its sister islands of St. Thomas and St. John, just 40 miles away. "We had our best tourism year since Hugo," said St. Croix's assistant tourism commissioner Jerry Koenke. Still, a "best year" does not automatically equate to overcrowding. In a normal year, some 1.5 million visitors, many of them onshore excursions from cruise ships, swamp tiny St. Thomas and tinier St. John, while just 370,000 visit far larger St. Croix—a source of its tranquility.

The summer and fall of 1995, when three huge storms hit land, will not soon be forgotten in the Caribbean and Gulf Coast regions. Hurricane Luis unleashed its fury on Antigua and Barbados, Marilyn blasted St. Thomas and St. John, and Opal, which is farther down the alphabet than hurricane names generally reach, slammed the Florida Panhandle and finally spent itself as a tropical storm. Following an earlier summer storm called Erin, which caused far less damage but may have lulled residents into a mistaken sense of security, Opal claimed 18 lives and caused $2 billion in property damage, largely along a 140-mile coastal stretch between Panama City, Florida, and Mobile, Alabama. This October storm ranks as the fourth most costly natural disaster in U.S. history.

capital of Willemstad one of the Caribbean's most enchanting cities. Bonaire, the midsize triplet, is the most natural of the three and has been designated in its entirety a marine park dedicated to protecting the underwater environment. As such, it is one of the world's leading scuba destinations.

Golf Comes to Aruba

Tierra del Sol, an 18-hole, par 71 golf course designed by Robert Trent Jones II, debuted in 1995. It is Aruba's first world-class golf course.

Bermuda

Though many people think of it as a Caribbean island, Bermuda is squarely in the Atlantic Ocean, 650 miles east of Cape Hatteras. This pristine paradise is the oldest British colony and the world's second oldest parliamentary democracy after England. Serene and stable with a semitropical climate and currency conveniently pegged to the U.S. dollar, Bermuda has long been a divine vacation destination and one of the hemisphere's most coveted honeymoon spots. Swimming, snorkeling, scuba diving, tennis, sailing, windsurfing, horseback riding, cycling and more golf courses per square mile than anyplace else on earth make Bermuda a grade-A destination. It seems as if it would also be the perfect place for a holiday home. However, unless you're extremely well-heeled, don't even consider it. Non-Bermudians are only permitted to purchase homes costing at least $1.7 million and condominiums priced at $350,000 or more, and only Bermudians are permitted to buy land.

KEEP IN MIND

➤ Tropical islands fall under various jurisdictions, meaning that regulations governing property ownership and taxation laws vary widely.

➤ You need to consider hurricanes in the Caribbean and Gulf of Mexico and typhoons in Hawaii when buying a vacation home.

➤ Large, more developed islands are easier to reach from the mainland, whereas smaller, less developed ones often require transferring to a commuter aircraft or even ferry.

CHAPTER 13

The Coast with the Most

The East Coast stretches from Florida to New England and boasts some of the world's best white-sand strands and a relatively temperate climate. The best beaches and the most enchanting communities are very likely to be on one of a chain of islands just offshore from the mainland. From Florida through the mid-Atlantic states, these islands tend to be long and thin—overgrown sand dunes, really—sculpted by the sea and the wind, anchored by tenacious flora and protective of the low-lying coastal mainland. They are called "barrier islands."

New England's coast is rockier, and seashore-lovers there have the choice of mainland or island beaches of considerable size or micro-beaches tucked into scenic, rock-rimmed coves. These alluring beaches are so much a part of the eastern consciousness that many citizens have long taken them for granted. Many people grew up in a family that had, or knew someone who had, a little beachfront bungalow that welcomed family and friends summer after summer.

We no longer take fabulous beaches for granted, to which many "save the shore" movements to protect the riparian environment testify. In addition to the importance of halting beach erosion and saving marine animals, the ante is up when it comes to the kind of property that people now consider a suitable second house for enjoying such a setting. Waterfront mansions may be a luxury of the past, but today's version of comfort isn't too shabby. If you're looking at coastal property or simply vacationing there, you won't be driving your father's Oldsmobile—and you won't be looking at the simple kind of place Aunt Mildred and Uncle Fred had. Quaint but rickety bungalows stocked with cast-off furniture from the primary residence are largely history, especially for anyone who wants a rental income. Instead of a cottage on Cape Cod, you might be looking at a wharfside condominium. The contemporary version of a house on the Jersey Shore, Delaware's Rehoboth Beach or Maryland's Ocean City might be a highrise condominium. Even if you find one of the originals, it might have been expanded, modernized or at least "charmed" to meet today's standards. And from the former potato fields of eastern Long Island to the "duney" barrier islands off the Carolinas, you'll also have a choice of designer homes, planned golf course communities or locations with either a dock in the backyard or easy access to boats.

Many people select their shore location based on where they live and work: Bostonians on Cape Cod, New Yorkers in the Hamptons, Philadelphians at the Jersey shore, Washingtonians at Rehoboth Beach and so on up and down the coast. If you live and/or work in or near one of these metro areas, you've probably spent some time at nearby shore resorts, and you'll probably want to consider one of these nearby coastal classics when you're shopping for a vacation home, especially if you plan to use it all or most weekends through the summer. You may be content with a nearby resort with sun and surf and perhaps the opportunity to play golf or tennis or to have a spot to tie up a boat. Ancillary diversions might be important to you too, especially if you're planning to rent your property out for part of the time and want to widen its potential appeal, or if you are ultimately thinking about retiring there.

GORGEOUS GEORGIA

Sandy beaches, humpbacked dunes, tidal washes, ponds and tenacious colonies of flora are the stuff Georgia's Golden Isles—and its barrier islands that spread northward for hundreds of miles—are made of. The Cumberland National Seashore on the southern reaches of the Georgia coast is a stringbean of an island, 16 miles long by 3 miles at its widest point. It is now pristine and protected, giving visitors a fine impression of what these coastal islands are like when they remain undeveloped. Alligators, sea turtles and some 300 species of herons, egrets, storks and other birds make this a naturalist's paradise. However, it was once a getaway Carnegie estate called Dungeness, and a trail to the ruins of the mansion gives an impression of what a retreat it was for the steel magnate.

Across the broad reaches of St. Andrews Sound is Jekyll Island, which was developed in the Carnegie era. A group of prominent families purchased this island in 1886 and developed it as a private resort. So it remained until World War II. Vanderbilts, Rockefellers, Morgans, Astors and similar families spent part of the year in opulent "cottages," 33 of which comprise the Jekyll Island Club Historic District. Jekyll Island is now far more egalitarian. Its four championship golf courses make it the largest public golf resort in the state and a 13-court municipal tennis center ranks with the best in the country. Fishing, water skiing, beaching, bicycling and playing in an 11-acre water park are also among Jekyll's diversions. Just 35 percent of the island is developed, with the remainder a natural preserve.

Similar low-key activities are the lure at neighboring Sea Island, which is known mainly as the site of an elegant, old-line Spanish-Mediterranean-style resort called The Cloister, which welcomes nonguests to admire its grounds and use the sports and dining facilities on a space-available basis. St. Simons is the shiniest of the Golden Isles and also the most developed. With a large selection of vacation homes and condominiums, shopping, entertainment and sports facilities, this Manhattan-sized barrier island offers a great variety of activities. All of these resort islands offer easy access to the 700-square-mile Okefenokee National Wildlife Refuge, a labyrinthian swampland of rivers, lakes and bogs, and habitat to abundant wildlife. Located inland on the Georgia-Florida border, Okefenokee is best seen by motorboat or canoe. The town of Waycross serves as the gateway to the refuge.

Savannah, tucked into the corner of Georgia closest to the South Carolina state line, is a beguiling city that epitomizes the Old South. This riverfront city grew wealthy as the South's cotton capital, and the best of antebellum architecture is on view. You can walk along streets shaded by live oaks, take a carriage ride and feel as if you've rolled back the decades, or see the sea on a paddlewheeler. Numerous parks dot the residential district and even the contemporary business area (Forrest Gump sat on a bench in one such park, dipping into his box of chocolates and waiting for his bus), while cobblestone and iron walkways give access to the old riverfront commercial district. A number of the finest mansions are open for touring, and when you visit, you'll feel as if you've stepped into the world of Scarlett and Rhett in their heyday.

Did You Know. . .

. . . that Savannah was preserved through the Civil War when locals, horrified at the fate that befell other cities as Union General William Sherman marched mercilessly through Georgia, surrendered rather than see their city destroyed?

COASTAL CAROLINA

From Hilton Head Island on the southern end of the state to Little River on the northern end, South Carolina's great beach resorts are among the nation's finest and most intensely developed. As you cross the state line from Savannah, you enter South Carolina's Low Country, a complex mesh of tidewater topography: sandy islands, tangled woodlands, cypress stands, marshes, rivers, salt creeks, bays and estuaries. These varied coastal habitats harbor sea turtles, hermit crabs, alligators, sandpipers, wild turkeys, deer, otter and scores of other species. Arguably the most famous resort community, one which kicked off the barrier island craze, is Hilton Head Island. Named for an English sea captain, not an American hotel baron, Hilton Head became the model for barrier island resort development, and the best resorts have drawn inspiration from it.

In 1956 a visionary developer named Charles Fraser foresaw the kind of community where people would want to live. He set his sights on Hilton Head, the second largest barrier island on the East Coast, and developed Sea Pines. This new brand of planned community was mindful of the natural wonders of its setting, yet provided a quality of life that became the model for scores of developments that followed. Sea Pines was carefully planned as a neighborhood in harmony with itself and its surroundings. In a sense, Fraser intuitively envisioned "ecotourism" before it had a name.

Sea Pines was Hilton Head's first development, but in the five short decades that followed Fraser's vision, the island skyrocketed to rarefied status as a presidential vacation spot. What was in the `50s a pioneering combination golf and beach resort on an off-the-beaten-path stretch of sand and scrub is today a vibrant destination where leisure and recreation have been refined to a high art. Island residents and visitors alike treasure the island's 15 golf courses (plus 4 more nearby just across the Calibogue Sound bridge in Bluffton on the mainland), plus tennis, water sports, boating, fishing, bicycling and wildlife viewing. The golf is world renowned, while Harbor Town is its peer among recreational boaters. The 4,000-acre Pickney Island Wildlife Refuge and Bluff Heritage Preserve protect wildlife habitats and are open to the public. While respecting nature, Hilton Head has grown into a harmonious planned community with an unsurpassed assortment of single-family homes, villas, condominiums and timeshares available for purchase, lease or short-term rental.

Did You Know. . .

. . . that Hilton Head Island has over 24,000 full-time residents (with a surprisingly low average age of 36) and 1.6 million visitors a year? Visitors have included President Bill Clinton and his family, who vacationed there in 1995.

Located on a deep natural harbor in the heart of the Low Country coast, Charleston is to South Carolina what Savannah is to Georgia: a splendidly preserved city of the antebellum South. It boasts such compelling attractions as glistening waterfront mansions along the Battery, grandiose plantations in the surrounding countryside, gussied-up eighteenth-century cotton and rice storehouses, lush parks and Fort Sumter, where the shots that set off the Civil War were fired on April 12, 1861. When you visit this gracious and gorgeous city, it is difficult to imagine its pivotal role in igniting the War Between the States, the bloodiest conflict in American military history. Charleston today is not just one of the country's top tourist destinations, but it has now spawned a number of nearby planned communities. You'll want to consider this region if you're attracted by the culture and beauty of the Old South with the recreation and lifestyle of the New.

Up the coast from Charleston is a region called the Tidelands of Georgetown that encompasses a peninsula between the Atlantic Ocean and Waccamaw River. The Atlantic side is the start of a 60-mile-long ribbon of white also known as the Grand Strand. Shopping, in both outlet stores and distinctive independent shops, is a major diversion in charming Georgetown and elsewhere in the region. Golfers have a choice of more than 80 courses, tennis players can select from over 500 courts, and the fishing is exceptional. Sightseers can stroll through picturesque towns or take boat rides, tram tours and even helicopter rides. The Georgetown Lighthouse is like a punctuation mark on the peninsula's southern end. The Waccamaw, which is part of the Intracoastal Waterway, and the nearby Pee Dee River were once the center of Carolina's famous rice country. Waterfowl have taken over abandoned ricefields, and the marshy rivers teem with channel bass, shrimp and crab. Litchfield Beach, Pawley's Island and Murrells Inlet are the leading coastal resort developments. Pawley's, in fact, lays claim to being the country's oldest beach resort, going back to when plantation owners fled the malaria-wracked interior. If you rent one of its quaint beach cottages, you'll probably find a Pawley's Island hammock on the porch. The island is now an especially popular winter escape for winter-weary Canadians.

Myrtle Beach, South Carolina's northeasternmost major resort area, may not be the oldest but it certainly has the greatest name recognition. That famous name now encompasses the seven communities (Murrells Inlet, Garden City Beach, Surfside Beach, Myrtle Beach, Atlantic Beach, North Myrtle Beach and Little River) that stretch along the Grand Strand's northern third. Intertwined with these traditional beach towns are newer residential communities, such as Litchfield by the Sea, Wilbrook, Myrtle Trace, Long Bay Club and Heritage Plantation. In addition to the ubiquitous recreational opportunities, the Myrtle Beach area is an entertainment center on the order of Nashville and Branson with 16,000 seats for live theater and music. The Carolina Opry, Alabama Theatre, Dolly Parton's Stampede, Gatlin Brothers Theatre and others pack them in.

South Carolina and North Carolina are neighbors and namemates, but their histories and geography have created different personalities. While South Carolina had waterfront cities and towns whose wealth came from nearby cotton, indigo and rice plantations, North Carolina's culture includes that of the Outer Banks' fishing villages, which developed their own distinctive culture. Another difference between the states is that South Carolina's barrier islands hug the coast, whereas North Carolina's Outer Banks thrust into the Atlantic farther offshore. This "hang-it-out" location, literally defying the ocean and oceanic storms, assured the Outer Banks a slower development and sense of gutsy isolation. The Sandhills in the state's deep coastal plain and the barrier islands are two popular getaways, and you'll find communities that range from extensively developed and modern to laid-back and traditional.

Top "Relo" Spots

A survey by the Center for Carolina Living of 15,000 families considering relocation to South Carolina revealed these to be the preferred towns:

1. Charleston*

2. Myrtle Beach*

3. Columbia

4. Greenville

5. Beaufort*

6. Hilton Head*

7. Spartanburg

8. Santee

9. Aiken

10. Georgetown*

*Seacoast communities

Just above the border with South Carolina, the Cape Fear area comprises North Carolina's southern coast—the part with a "bump" on the map where the shoreline veers from its strong eastward orientation to a more northeasterly one. Wilmington, a former cotton port, has been revitalized and is now the showplace of this once-neglected stretch. It has become a town of festivals showcasing everything from azaleas to jazz. Wilmington is also the port of the battleship *North Carolina* and site of a good railroad museum. Carolina, Kure and Wrightsville are the best beaches, and surf fishing vies with sunbathing and swimming as the favorite activity.

The Outer Banks are something else, a combination of historic hamlets, newer vacation homes and huge expanses of protected land that give residents and vacationers alike real breathing room. Cape Lookout National Seashore and Cape Hatteras National Seashore are glorious strips of sand. The 208-foot Cape Hatteras lighthouse is the tallest in the United States and with good reason. Early navigators soon learned to avoid the Outer Banks and their ship-eating shoals, which were known as the "Graveyard of the Atlantic." Yesterday's tragedies have turned into today's recreation as some 600 known shipwrecks are a natural habitat for fish, making the Outer Banks one of the eastern coast's preeminent scuba diving and fishing areas.

The Outer Banks owe their sparse population to isolation, while the aptly named Sandhills owe their late growth to soil that was not sought after by early farmers. Though in the coastal plain and therefore firmly in North Carolina's interior, the Sandhills were once Atlantic beaches. The region's center is a historic town called Southern Pines, but the development of spectacular year-round golfing in nearby Pinehurst puts this quaint, New England-style town on the map with the great coastal resorts. In fact, Pinehurst has become synonymous with great golf. In early 1996, the number of courses was an imposing 38 with 6 more under construction—an impressive percentage of North Carolina's statewide total of more than 500 golf courses.

Did You Know. . .

. . . that the Pinehurst Country Club, founded in 1895, is the world's largest golf resort? It is operated by the Dallas-based Club Corporation of America (CCA), which operates 260 of the country's top private clubs (owning a handful of them) and has more than 400,000 members who view CCA operation as a guarantee that its member courses offer style, quality, amenities and service.

MID-ATLANTIC MECCAS

Chesapeake Bay notches into the mainland from Virginia's Norfolk-Newport News harbor to Maryland's Havre de Grace-Aberdeen, which are practically in the corner where the state butts up against Delaware and Pennsylvania. This huge bay and the rivers that feed it are a huge and threatened ecosystem. Historically one of the nation's richest fishing, oystering and crabbing areas, the Chesapeake's tilt has become decidedly recreational and increasingly residential. The bay remains one of America's preeminent sailing areas, with open stretches of water and protective harbors and coves. The shore areas closest to major cities have increasingly been suburbanized, while second-home developments are springing up in more distant areas.

The Delmarva Peninsula, shared by Delaware, Maryland, and Virginia, still retains some of its original rural flavor. Each of these three states has one major seaside resort grown to major proportions with plenty of accommodations—from cottages to condominiums—and entertainment aplenty. The trio is composed of Virginia Beach, Virginia; Ocean City, Maryland; and Rehoboth Beach, Delaware. Maryland's is the largest portion of the peninsula. Residents refer to it as the Eastern Shore, and much of it is still so rural and remote that, despite its short distance from Washington, it was considered a suitably out-of-the-way spot for the 1995 Israeli-Syrian peace negotiations. Chincoteague and Assateague are the Eastern Shore's major barrier islands, largely protected as national seashore and state park land.

Did You Know. . .

. . . that New Jersey has the highest portion of waterfront and coastline of any of the mainland's 48 states and the second-largest in the U.S. after Hawaii? The western border is the 180-mile Delaware River. To the east are the Atlantic Ocean, Raritan and New York Bays, and the Hudson River. That leaves just the Garden State's 50-mile northern boundary with New York as a land-only state border.

New Jersey's 127-mile coast, also known as the Jersey Shore, has long been the summer escape for residents of steamy Philadelphia, New York and other Middle Atlantic cities. Cape May, at the southern tip of New Jersey, is a Victorian jewel. Once the playground of presidents, it now draws admirers of homes adorned with gingerbread fretwork and other ornamentation popularized a century ago. Jersey Shore communities slide along the scale from opulent to ordinary, with properties ranging from mansions to timeshares. Boardwalks abound, and the beaches, many of them for the private use of residents and renters, are outstanding. Like the Chesapeake Bay communities, some are now becoming commuter suburbs or exurbs. Bay Head, Belmar, Long Branch, Ocean Grove, Rumson, Bradley Beach and Spring Lake are highly developed, each with its own style and habitués. While not within easy commuting distance of New York, Philadelphia or Trenton, the string of beach communities from Barnegat Light to Beach Haven on Long Island offers varied housing styles and prices. In many ways, all the other places on the Shore pale in comparison to Atlantic City, which underwent a renaissance with the advent of casino gambling in the early '80s. It has been a selective renaissance, however, with glitzy casino-hotels along the Boardwalk and bay sides, and parking lots and wastelands behind and between.

If suburb had a prototype, it would be Long Island, whose housing tracts stretch endlessly from Queens through Nassau County and well into Suffolk. Only in Suffolk's far reaches, where the island forks into two branches, do true vacation homes blossom along sandy beaches and in former potato fields and sheltered bays. This whole glamorous neighborhood is "the Hamptons," known as much for its chic as its opulent old mansions and new designer dwellings. Sunning, shopping, dining, waiting for a table to dine, seeing and being seen sum up much of today's Hampton style—at least in summer. Breezy, fragrant springs and clear, crisp falls stretch the season, and for many people are the finest time of all.

NEW ENGLAND HIGHLIGHTS

Rhode Island

The south coast of New England, particularly such towns as Watch Hill and Newport, Rhode Island, were traditional summer watering holes for East Coast society. Beautifully located on a peninsula between Narragansett Bay and the Atlantic, Newport has been treated well by the centuries. Its eighteenth-century historic core is one of the nation's best-preserved colonial centers, while the opulent Gilded Age mansions lining the Cliff Walk overlooking Easton Bay and the ocean are America's answer to the Loire chateau country of France. Several of the finest mansions are open to tours, including The Breakers, a sumptuous palace designed by society architect Richard Morris Hunt for Cornelius Vanderbilt, and Hammersmith Farm, where John F. Kennedy and Jacqueline Bouvier were married. Until it lost the venue to San Diego, Newport long hosted the America's Cup and is still the site of other prestigious yacht races. It also sponsors a season's worth of music festivals, tennis tournaments, fishing tournaments and art shows.

Block Island, accessible only by ferry or air, is an old fishing island off the Rhode Island coast that for two centuries slumbered in virtual isolation. With the advent of the steamship in the mid-nineteenth century, Block Island became a summer haven, and its architecture and spirit reflect the growth spurt of the late 1800s. Fishing, beachcombing, bicycle touring and simply relaxing remain the primary diversions on this restful island.

Massachusetts

The East Coast has other capes—Cape Fair, Cape Hatteras, Cape May—but for Bostonians and other New Englanders, only one counts. When they say "the Cape," they are talking about Cape Cod and no other. This curved peninsula muscles its way from the Massachusetts coast south of Boston, resembling nothing so much as a Brobdingnagian flexed arm. You may prefer the beach side or the bay side, but each has its own appeal. The beaches and marshes are still achingly beautiful, especially in the off-season, but some of the towns have mushroomed into small cities as more and more vacationers, urban weekenders, second-home owners, and a growing colony of year-round residents pile onto the Cape. With city-style peak-season traffic, especially on Route 6, the bicycle is a "primo" mode of transportation on this flat, sandy peninsula.

Yet despite its meteoric growth, Cape Cod's appeal has never dimmed. Sandwich on the bay side has lovely sheltered beaches and an excellent museum showcasing glassware. Falmouth, across the widest part of the Cape on the south shore, is a charming little city in tandem with neighboring Wood's Hole. Wood's Hole—the center of American oceanic research—has several laboratories and institutes, some of which are open to the public. When Japan's late emperor, the scientifically inclined Hirohito, visited the United States in 1976, he especially requested a stop there.

Wood's Hole is the prime jumping-off point for Martha's Vineyard, a chic offshore island just a 45-minute ferry ride from the mainland. It is New England's largest island with dramatic coastal cliffs, gorgeous beaches, sheltering harbors, pine forests and seven towns; Edgartown is the largest town but it's not large at all. "The Vineyard" has seen its share of celebrity—and notoriety. The late Jacqueline Kennedy Onassis,

Art Buchwald, Walter Cronkite, Alan Dershowitz, Mia Farrow, Spike Lee, and other notables have or had summer homes on Martha's Vineyard, finding as much privacy and seclusion as they wished; and in their early White House years, the Clintons too vacationed there. The neighboring island of Chappaquiddick and its infamous bridge will always serve as a footnote to history. That's where Massachusetts Senator Edward Kennedy drove into the water, drowning both his passenger Mary Jo Kopechne and his chance for the presidency.

When the Kennedys installed themselves in their family compound at Hyannisport, the Cape was still relatively secluded and quiet. Now nearby Hyannis has grown into a major commercial and shopping center, known more for services than for tranquility. Yarmouth Port, Chatham, Orleans and Eastham are mid-Cape communities awash with a combination of history and modern developments and all close to outstanding beaches. The Cape Cod National Seashore, comprising the entire shore between Chatham and Provincetown, was President Kennedy's legacy to preserve a portion of the Cape he so loved. In 1961 he created an area of 44,000 acres of ocean beaches, dunes, and salt ponds protected from development. Swimming, sunning, cycling, nature trails and bridle paths make the seashore an oasis. Wellfleet and its attractive harbor on the bay is the main town on the narrowing portion of the Cape.

The contrast between the National Seashore and Provincetown on the tip of the Cape is dramatic. With great beaches on both sides of the land and a wonderful harbor from which whale-watching cruises now depart, "P-town" is built on a foundation of stiff-lipped New England tradition (Pilgrims, seafarers, whalers, fishermen and all that) overlaid with an artistic gloss. The Provincetown Players is one of the country's preeminent summer theaters; in addition to art galleries, studios, fine restaurants and hip shops are up-to-the-minute clubs, cafes and bars that keep the town hopping long after most of New England is asleep.

Nantucket is a two-and-a-half-hour ferry ride from Hyannis or the Vineyard. This compact island, nicknamed "the Little Grey Lady of the Sea," maintains its maritime ambiance. The Nantucket style is one of quaint, gray-shuttered cottages often adorned with trellises of roses that bloom with particular abandon. Nantucket's breeze-kissed beaches, heaths, meadows and salt marshes have the power to energize and tranquilize.

Maine

Maine is roughly the size of the five other New England states combined. Its coastline is one of the most beautiful and rugged stretches of seashore anywhere on this earth. The road distance from Kittery on the New Hampshire state line to Eastport at the Canadian border is 293 miles, but if you ironed out Maine's coves, bays and rockheads, it would be more like 3,500 miles of coastline. Your dream of a vacation and ideal spot for a vacation home may be an old fishing village, a secluded island, an old farmhouse a few miles inland or an oceanfront condominium, and Maine gives you that choice. Ogunquit is one of the prettiest ocean towns, while neighboring Kennebunkport, another charmer where George and Barbara Bush and their brood summered, is on the southern coast.

Portland, just a few miles to the north, is Maine's largest city. Its revitalized harbor and downtown area are a fitting introduction to the spirit and history of Maine. It is the site of such museums as the Wadsworth-Longfellow House (the boyhood home of the poet), the Tate House (built by George Tate, who made a fortune selling sturdy Maine trees to the British for ships' masts), and the Victoria Mansion (with one of the best collections of Victoriana on the coast). The Portland Museum of Art boasts a noteworthy collection of eighteenth- and nineteenth-century American works, and the waterfront galleries are where you can buy your own twentieth-century treasures.

Did You Know. . .

. . . that the coast of Maine has 63 lighthouses, including the Portland Head Light, which was commissioned by George Washington?

Shoppers also flock to Maine, notably Freeport, which is just a few miles north of Portland. Freeport owes its status as a "gonzo" shopping district to L. L. Bean. This old-fashioned country store stayed open around the clock to supply fishermen in the days when the rest of New England turned in with the chickens. Bean's has grown into a mammoth catalog and retail operation specializing in sporty clothing, outdoor gear and backcountry sports equipment. But one thing has not changed: Bean's is still open 24 hours a day, seven days a week. It has spawned a retail culture—name-brand factory outlets line the once quiet town and shoppers are as abundant as mosquitoes around a marsh.

Mt. Desert Island has the greatest concentration of attractions along the coast. You might be more familiar with the name Bar Harbor, the island's fabled resort town. While the Roosevelts bought Campobello, other social families elected to build mansions around the picturesque port town of Bar Harbor. Many of these mansions were destroyed by fire in 1947, but those remaining give the island an old-fashioned cachet. Bar Harbor continues to delight visitors, and many also visit for the natural beauty of Acadia National Park—the only national park in New England, one of the few east of the Mississippi and the second most-visited in the United States.

The Roosevelts of Hyde Park summered grandly on Campobello Island, which is officially located in Canadian waters but is accessed from Lubec, Maine. The vacation "cottage" where Franklin Roosevelt was diagnosed with polio is now part of Roosevelt Campobello International Park, a 2,600-acre nature preserve and historic site that is well worth the long trip to the far corner of "down east."

KEEP IN MIND

➤ A seaside home located to take advantage of prevailing breezes minimizes the need for air-conditioning in spring and fall. A protective roof will shelter the home's interior from the scorching summer sun, while location, suitable materials and clever use of verandas can provide passive solar heat to pare winter utility bills.

➤ If you love to garden, the virtually guaranteed zone of no freezes from the Carolinas south provides the longest growing season.

➤ Coastal climate is moderated by saltwater. Summers will be cooler and winters milder near saltwater than an inland location at the same latitude.

CHAPTER 14

South of the Border

A *mañana* mentality and a place where money goes far and margaritas flow may be reason enough to select a vacation destination, especially when you're there to scout for a second home. But once the relaxing glow of a slow-paced lifestyle and the novelty of a budget locale wear off, you might want more. Some of Latin America's top resorts have become escapes where second homes often have retirement potential. If that's what you're scouting for, you may want a livelier place with facilities and services that enable you to be there year-round. Then again, you probably want a place that's not *too* lively. Political stability and an attitude of *gringo* acceptance should be high on the list of criteria for places in Latin America that you consider.

MEXICO

Mexico City is the country's political, financial and cultural capital, but major tourist centers are on the coasts and in the cool mountains. Because they are such fine winter escapes, rates actually drop during the summer months. Many larger resort cities have designated a "hotel zone" or "tourist zone" with a concentration of lodgings, restaurants, shops and nightspots to appeal to foreign visitors, and each has its own airport.

Rethinking Crime Figures

Three of the countries with the lowest rates of reported crimes, according to the U.S. National Bureau of Interpol, defy the stereotypes of dangerous countries. In the category of reported crimes are homicide, rape and other sex offenses, serious assault, and various kinds of theft, including aggravated or violent theft, robbery, breaking and entering, and automobile theft. These statistics are for *reported* crimes, which may be just the tip of the proverbial iceberg, but they still bear consideration, especially in contrast with what we think of as "civilized" first-world countries, as reported in the September 1995 issue of *International Living.*

Mexico	71 per 100,000 people
Honduras	125
Thailand	159
Costa Rica	173
Great Britain	3,239
France	4,632
United States	5,482
Australia	5,549
New Zealand	9,485

Acapulco put Mexico's Pacific coast on the map as a major tourist destination. Its benign year-round climate and stunning location around a huge bay made it a fairytale retreat in the '40s. However, explosive growth (the population now exceeds two million), haphazard construction, and the jet-age emergence of quieter, better-designed resorts have turned it into more of a tour-group and convention center than a vacation resort.

Puerto Vallarta picked up where Acapulco left off. Once a sleepy haven snuggled between the Sierra Madre and Bahia de Banderas (Mexico's largest bay), Puerto Vallarta was catapulted to international renown when Elizabeth Taylor and Richard Burton dallied there during the filming of *Night of the Iguana.* The center of the city is a well-preserved, spruced-up version of what was there in 1964 when the movie was made. Pastel buildings with red tile roofs line the cobblestone streets, and brilliant bougainvillea vines threaten to take over every city wall. The booming resort's 25 miles of beaches are captivating; and opportunities for swimming, sailing, golf, tennis and fishing abound.

The success of Acapulco first and later of Puerto Vallarta has set off a chain reaction among other coastal towns. Charles Kurlander writes in his book *West Mexico from Sea to Sierra* that "Mazatlán has cleaner beaches than Acapulco, more preserved history than Puerto Vallarta, and is cheaper, more convenient to ferry, train, and road than any other resort in Mexico." What a nutshell full of pluses! Located north of Acapulco on a peninsula that sticks out into the Pacific Ocean, Mazatlán also boasts one of the longest uninterrupted stretches of beach in the country. Sport fishing is legendary, and facilities for water sports, golf and tennis tend to be less pressured than in other Mexican resorts.

Did You Know. . .

. . . that Mexico has turned resort development into a home-grown industry and has become the model for developing countries with fledgling tourist industries? FONATUR is a national trust charged with expanding and promoting Mexico's tourist infrastructure. Since the early 1970s, the agency has overseen the development of Cancun, Los Cabos, Ixtapa/Zihuatanejo, Huatulco and Loreta. FONATUR seeks undeveloped areas where it is feasible to create the infrastructure for sustainable growth while being environmentally sensitive—another way of saying water, sewage, telephone and electrical systems. The agency began by financing new hotel construction and rehabilitation and has more recently embarked on developing self-contained tourist villages with hotels, private homes, marinas, sports facilities and shops.

When FONATUR comes in, you'll hear a boom.

Ixtapa and Zihuatanejo, paired villages just four miles apart, are located on an isolated coastal stretch nicknamed "the Riviera of Mexico." That name is an insult, however, because Palmar Beach is longer and far sandier than anything you're likely to find on France's Mediterranean coast. Ixtapa, one of Mexico's more recent master-planned resorts, boasts golf courses, a fine yacht harbor and the usual resort assortment of water and land sports. Zihuatanejo is an older town, a true Mexican fishing community that has adapted to being a tourist center as well.

The Bay of Huatulco is the southernmost beach resort on Mexico's Pacific Coast. Its 18 miles of beaches were once the site of a couple of fishing villages only. Then came Las Hadas, a glamorous hideaway resort accessible only to the moneyed. More recently, FONATUR (see box) has been pouring money into and support behind the development of a large resort to rival Acapulco and Cancun in size and scale. Golf, marinas, water sports facilities and shops join hotels and residential areas to create a sparkling new destination.

There Are Angels, and They're Green

Driving in Latin America has a reputation for being, to put it kindly, problematic. Obstacle-filled secondary roads, the very real possibility of banditry (or at least larceny) in case of a breakdown, and the scarcity of U.S.-style service stations can be daunting. Mexico's Green Angels are an ingenious solution for tourists in trouble on the road.

More than a thousand Green Angels patrol 230 popular routes around the country, totaling some 30,000 road miles. They operate service centers and mobile radio vehicles and repair vans, offering free help to stranded motorists, RV operators and even bus drivers.

The desert peninsula of Baja California is longer than Italy. The Pacific Ocean is to the west and the Sea of Cortes (which you may know as the Gulf of California) to the east. At Baja's southernmost tip lie Los Cabos, a cluster of resort centers that are a sunlover's playground. San Jose del Cabo and Cabo San Lucas are fast-growing resorts. Sun, sand, and sea sports from sport fishing to scuba diving have been Los Cabos staples, and significant golf and tennis resorts have most recently been added. La Playita, Palmilla, Cabo del Sol, Cabo Real, Campa de Carlos and Puerto Los Cabos are the newest developments, which are making Los Cabos something akin to the Hilton Head Island of Mexico.

Cancun and nearby Cozumel are the opposite numbers on the east coast of the Yucatán Peninsula. Cancun was the first of Mexico's planned tourist centers. In two decades, it has mushroomed into a popular Miami-style highrise resort—too big for some but just right for many. Cancun offers city-style scale and services with resort atmosphere and amenities. The Yucatán is also the site of two of the most famous and accessible Mayan sites, inland Chichen-Itza and coastal Tulum.

Akumal and Playa del Carmen are smaller, quieter, lesser-known beach towns. The offshore island of Cozumel, by contrast, is also small, but it isn't quiet and it is world famous. Cozumel is a low-lying island with one lively town (San Miguel) and is world renowned as a diving destination because of a chain of legendary reefs of such scale and grandeur that even Jacques-Yves Cousteau was impressed.

Sometimes you may be a beach "nut"; sometimes you're not. For those not-nut times, Mexico's great colonial cities make for fascinating inland vacationing. Guadalajara is Mexico's second largest city, site of Latin America's largest covered market with a climate that has been described as "12 months of springtime." Guanojuato, the richest of the colonial silver towns, is now a pedestrian-friendly center of traditional architecture and one of the country's most important art centers (muralist Diego Rivera was born there). UNESCO declared Morelia a World Heritage Artistic Site for its wealth of colonial buildings surrounded by pine-clad mountainsides, waterfalls and a galaxy of small satellite villages. San Miguel de Allende is a cosmopolitan and artsy city, also known as an American retirement colony. Many residents came to visit and were captivated by the city's beauty and charm. Perhaps you will be too.

CENTRAL AMERICA

The current boom in Central American tourism can be summarized in two words: Costa Rica. This environmentally conscious, politically stable and peaceful country has been nicknamed "the Switzerland of Central America." Ecotourists have been on the forefront of the influx into this stunning country, home to 800 species of birds (more than in all of North America), 300 species of reptiles, and some 10 percent of the world's butterflies species—and to a population that respects and protects nature. The capital of San José nestles in the Central Highlands, a volcanic range. National parks abound. Inland activities include rafting, cycling, hiking and birdwatching, while Caribbean and

Pacific centers enable visitors to enjoy beaches, fishing, scuba diving and windsurfing.

Belize, the former British Honduras, is a small, politically progressive nation that has drawn its inspiration from Costa Rica for environmental policies. Boasting the three Rs of Latin American tourist attractions—reefs, ruins and rain forests—it's both compact and fascinating. Flora and fauna are the keys to enjoying Belize's natural abundance, but they'll vie for your attention with such significant Mayan ruins as Caracol, Xuantich, Lamanani and Uxbenton. Belize is also noted for its Caribbean sand beaches and fabulous reefs for scuba diving.

Honduras is another country trying to jump aboard the ecotourism bandwagon. With a long Caribbean coastline, a short Pacific one, cloud forests, rain forests, jungles and more than 70 wildlife preserves and other protected areas, this congenial country has a good start. Copan, in northwestern Honduras close to the Guatemalan border, is one of the top Mayan centers. Massively excavated and reconstructed but still not completed, it is a mecca for art lovers, amateur archaeologists and those who are touched by the craftsmanship and wonder of the ancient world. If you dive, you'll want to head to the Bay Islands, located on the southeastern end of the world's second longest barrier reef (Belize's top diving sites are on the northwestern end of the same reef system).

Panama, El Salvador and Guatemala are fascinating countries, but travelers have by and large been scared off by political problems. Even in times of strife, intrepid travelers with special interests sometimes make a dash for one particular site—perhaps the Mayan city of Tikal in northeastern Guatemala; the art centers of Ilobasco or San Vicente in El Salvador; the Masaya area with a major market, a volcano and a national park with the same name in Nicaragua; or the Panama Canal, which slices through the country. But a new emphasis on tourist development, increased stability and safety throughout the region, and a search for new travel horizons may put these countries in your future agenda.

KEEP IN MIND

➤ Although Spanish is overwhelmingly the language of Mexico and Central America (many moderately priced Spanish immersion courses are available), English is widely spoken in resorts. English-speaking pockets also exist in Belize and the Bay Islands of Honduras.

➤ One of the benefits of owning a vacation home in this part of the world is that cooks, gardeners, housekeepers, baby-sitters and other help are easily available and affordable.

➤ Fine fruits and vegetables are available at local markets, but remember to use bottled water to wash produce, to drink and even to brush your teeth.

PART FOUR

The ABCs of Purchasing and Profiting from Your Home

CHAPTER 15

Paying for the Place You Want

You've narrowed down the type of home you want, even the community. Now you're ready—eager—to buy. You may wonder why Chapter 15 concerns itself with paying for your home and Chapter 16 begins the househunt. Isn't that the reverse of the proper order?

Not at all. You'll need to work on some numbers before seriously looking at leisure properties so you'll know your price range and so you and the real estate agent who will be assisting you won't waste time going through homes well beyond your limit. If you'll be financing your second-home purchase, there are steps to take now to make that process flow smoothly into a completed sale.

IT'S NOT JUST THE MORTGAGE

In calculating what amount of loan payment you can carry for a second home, along with the mortgage for your principal residence and real estate taxes, you'll have to include the costs of maintaining that vacation place where the dollars can fly out the window. Homes in oceanfront communities take a beating from the elements, both winter and summer, and require constant repairs. So can ski places. So can any home that has tenants moving in and out.

You may be surprised at the money you'll have to spend each year just for the upkeep of your getaway without even getting into improvements and new installations.

If you need and expect rentals to pay for much of your vacation-home expense—mortgage, property taxes, insurance, utilities, repairs—you'll have to be especially careful when you buy. Make certain you choose a place in a resort community where renting is likely to be no problem. There are no guarantees, of course, but the "hot" area is obviously going to attract more vacationers than the out-of-the-way spot.

If you're looking at your home for your enjoyment only and have no plans to rent, then the potential rentability aspect of househunting and the property you buy will not apply to you (but the expenses of upkeep and repairs will!).

Think about "what ifs" too. If you're able to rent only half as often as you would like, could you still carry the house financially? What if it were damaged and you were unable to rent it for a while? Could you still meet payments? We're not talking *profit* here, just meeting ongoing expenses.

PAYING CASH

Some 30 to 40 percent of buyers do pay cash for a leisuretime property. That could be because there are a lot of wealthy people buying second homes, but another reason is because many of those properties are inexpensively priced. With a large number of vacation houses and condominiums carrying price tags of $50,000 or less, a high percentage of shoppers can—and choose to—write a check and pay outright.

Some take the money from savings, whereas others refinance their principal home and draw out some or much of the equity for the down payment. Naturally, that makes the mortgage amount higher, which admittedly is not exactly the same as paying cash from money that had been in savings. Still, the second home *is* free of debt, and debt is consolidated into the primary residence's mortgage.

Should you cash in some securities to pay for your home, or would it be wiser to take out a mortgage? The mortgage interest is, after all, tax deductible. Personal elements, plus your own particular financial profile, enter into that decision. By all means talk with your tax advisor.

Refinancing News

It used to be that refinancing a mortgage made sense only if interest rates had dropped at least two percentage points below the rate you held. Financial experts say now, however, that many lenders have eliminated or reduced the fees known as points, so it can pay to switch to more favorable terms whenever they present themselves if you plan to stay in that home for several years.

THE SECOND-HOME MORTGAGE

If you must, or want to, secure a loan for a second-home purchase, there's much information you'll want, and need, to know about the market today.

Second-home loans can be harder to secure than mortgages for a principal residence. But remember, more than half of all buyers do finance their homes, so the loans are out there. Here are some points to consider and cautions to weigh when you think mortgage.

- If you own where you live now, your vacation-home loan will be a first mortgage on another piece of real estate, not a second mortgage.
- If you rent where you live now, your loan will still be considered a mortgage for a vacation home, complete with cautions lenders still have toward such properties.
- Mortgage interest rates are likely to be .5 to 1 percent higher on vacation homes than they are for primary residences. Again, that's because lenders consider these properties a greater risk to them than a principal home.
- One source of a loan could be the home seller, who might not need a lump sum of cash from the sale as the owner of a principal home would. Sellers figure more prominently in vacation-home financing than they do in selling a primary residence.
- If you're buying into a new-home community, the developer might help with financing. The developer's terms are likely to be a little higher than borrowing through a traditional lender, so by all means shop around before committing yourself to that financing.

- Shopping around should include calling several local lenders, local meaning in the area of the vacation property. No lender miles away from that home is going to be interested in lending you money. An exception might be a lender in your permanent community—a bank or other lending institution—that has a branch office in your resort area. An exception is sometimes made, too, if you are a *very* good, long-standing customer of a lending institution in your year-round town.
- Something to think about here: If your lender in your Illinois hometown says, "Sure, we'll give you a loan for a Florida home," be certain you know the expenses that mortgage will entail. The lender might, for example, be totally unfamiliar with Florida's real estate laws and will engage an attorney and appraiser there before approving your loan—charges that will be passed on to you.
- You can shop the Internet. Most on-line services have mortgage information available from a variety of sources, companies that will happily drown you in paper and numbers.
- Your real estate agent can help with many of your financing questions, but keep in mind the agent probably deals with one or two lenders almost exclusively, and they may not have the best rates. You'll still be wise to shop around.

Preapproval

This is a smart step to take before seriously househunting because, as we mentioned, it helps define your financial picture and allows you to know the price range of the home that lenders will believe you can afford and, second, real estate agents sometimes won't show homes to shoppers who aren't preapproved, both for their sake and the sake of the buyer. These days, preapproval saves everyone time.

Being *preapproved* differs from being *prequalified* for a loan. You might see the latter term often when reading about mortgages. With preapproval you have a real lender—bank, savings and loan, credit union and the like—that gives you a written statement to the effect that that institution will offer you a mortgage for a specific amount at a specified rate of interest for a specified period of time. Two contingencies usually apply: a satisfactory appraisal of the home you choose by that lender and reverification of the information on your loan application, which could change in the few months between preapproval and your actually buying the house.

You can secure a mortgage preapproval when you make a formal application for a loan even though you don't yet have a home selected. The stages of a loan application are the same as if you were applying *after* finding a place—income and savings verification, credit check and so on.

A *prequalifying document,* on the other hand, is simpler. It indicates what your income is and states that if you make "x" dollars a year, you should be able to buy a home for "y" dollars. But the lender does not take into account your current debt load and credit report—factors considered before approval is granted. And you are not promised a loan by the institution. So what good is that paper? Good question. It really promises or guarantees you and the lender nothing at all.

Some Nightstand Reading

An important element in your being approved for a mortgage is what your credit report says about you. It is wise to send for a copy before a lender sees it so you can clear up any mistakes. Check the Yellow Pages under "Credit Reporting Agencies" to find the one that has you on file. You can expect to pay anywhere from $2 to $25 for a copy of that document.

If you find a mistake in your report, work with the credit bureau until you're satisfied that it has been corrected.

Looking to a Mortgage Broker

A particularly smart approach to second-home financing is looking into the services of a mortgage broker. This is an individual or firm that arranges, or brokers, mortgage loans for homebuyers with a financial institution that offers the best rates and terms for that particular buyer. When you work with a mortgage broker, you might actually have applied to a wide range of lenders, from Citicorp, GMAC, Chase Manhattan Bank and other major institutions to innumerable smaller, lesser-known ones. The services of a mortgage broker are not all that well known, but they make many, many a match between a buyer and lender.

Notes Carolyn Janik, a New England real estate agent and author of several books on home buying and selling: "Mortgage brokers can be especially helpful with a second home, since some local lenders—in your principal-home community or in the second-home locale—might not be too eager to make those loans. In a down economy when workers are losing their jobs, those lenders are often left with second-home foreclosures sooner than they are for principal homes."

Homebuyers' costs for utilizing a mortgage broker vary. Sometimes there is no fee—the broker is paid by the lending institution making the loan. Or when that's not the case, a househunter might be charged a minimal negotiated fee.

You can find these specialists through the Yellow Pages. Look under "Mortgages" for companies or individuals with the words *mortgage broker* in their advertising. They might also note in their advertisement their membership in a statewide or national association for brokers—another way to spot these specialists.

THE MORTGAGE ITSELF

For a few years now we have enjoyed very low rates of interest on home loans—under 8 percent for a fairly long time. These low rates are expected to continue, at least barring a major economic shake-up.

The spread is narrow now between a fixed-rate loan and an adjustable rate mortgage (ARM). However, if rates rise, that very attractive ARM introductory rate will jump, usually two percentage points, with a lifetime cap of six points.

If you're planning to keep your home for perhaps only four or five years, the ARM could be a better way to go as its first-year rate can be lower than a fixed-rate loan. If you plan to stay in your home a long time, the fixed rate might make more sense. What you need here is a mortgage-table book with an amortization table. These small paperbacks can be found in bookstores with such titles as *Mortgage Payments* or *Mortgage Payment Guide*. Dig out your calculator and see just how much you might save with a fixed rate and with an ARM.

Much of the financing for a second home is similar to that for a primary residence—jumbo loans, for example, or points charged. A point equals 1 percent of the loan amount, and you could be charged one, two or more points. Lenders use points to increase the yield of the loan. While you may get a .5 percent lower interest rate, say, with three points charged you, you could pay more in the long run. Get out that calculator again and you will probably find the .5 percent reduction is no bargain and you would do better paying the three points at a .5 percent higher interest rate.

Some aspects of borrowing for a second home, on the other hand, are different. For example, you cannot secure Federal Housing Administration (FHA)-backed or Veterans Administration (VA)-backed financing for a vacation home as you may be able to for a primary residence.

You also do not qualify for a mortgage on a second home with state-sponsored mortgage programs that offer lower-than-market interest rates and low down payments—programs intended to assist primary home owners.

THE DOWN PAYMENT

The amount you'll need to put down on your leisure home is usually higher than that required for a principal residence. You're likely to be asked for as much as a 20, or even 30, percent down payment.

Where will that money come from? Perhaps from savings, or you might secure a home equity loan on your primary residence, the interest from which is tax deductible. Be very careful about your ability to repay all of that debt load every month (although of course the lender will take your obligations into account when deciding whether you can carry the added burden of a second-home loan).

KEEP IN MIND

➤ Besides paying for your second home, factor in the expense of maintaining and repairing it.

➤ Be certain you can afford to carry the house or apartment financially if rentals you were counting on should fall through.

➤ Talk with your financial adviser about the wisdom of paying cash for your home versus mortgaging the property.

➤ Mortgage interest rates and down payment requirements are higher for vacation homes than for primary residences.

CHAPTER 16

At Last—Buying the Home That's Perfect for You

Now that your financing situation has been clarified, it's time to shop for that splendid second home, the one out there with your name on it.

Let's take this one step at a time, exactly as you'll move through the buying process.

CHECKING OUT A NEIGHBORHOOD

That magic real estate word *location* applies to vacation-home communities, too, but perhaps there is less chance of making a wrong location decision when you're dealing with a desirable resort town. Still, many resorts do have a "wrong side of the tracks."

Should you buy there just to have a Sandy Dunes postal address? W-e-l-l-l-l, that depends.

Perhaps the blocks in question are simply modest compared to other parts of town but are well maintained. That's not risky. But if the neighborhood is run-down, you could be buying into a continuing slide. Yes, you might be the start of a renovation movement in that enclave, but what if no one follows you? Or how many years will it take to turn it all around? Unless rehabilitation is already well underway in the blocks that interest you, your best bet for financial safety is the established part of the town or the modest-but-neat neighborhood.

If you are condominium shopping, there's more to take into account. Aside from the condo complex that's simple versus the one with bells and whistles—a personal choice likely to be determined by what you can afford—here are important points to consider, neighborhood-wise.

Is the condo community that interests you well maintained? The slightest sign of neglect could mean there isn't enough money in the coffers to pay for landscaping, exterior painting and other repairs or upgrades. If a unit there seems like a bargain, it isn't a bargain if the entire complex is slipping. Remember, you are tied in with the whole condo community. If it runs down, so does your investment.

One point to keep in mind when neighborhood shopping: Look for something special. Do those blocks—or the home you like in them—have a great view of the lake? A golf course? Having only one unique feature can be an attraction for tenants that could separate you from homeowners with more ordinary properties.

For Maximum Effect

If you want a better guarantee of having your condo apartment rented when you'd like it to be than merely management's or a local real estate agency's say-so, check this: Is your resort complex associated with a travel agency or national network that markets resort condos around the country—perhaps around the world—to Americans looking for a condo vacation? That rental strategy is likely to bring the greatest number of tenants your way. You can't try to rent your own unit this way because it takes the numbers an entire condo resort provides.

When buying a condominium in a year-round community, you should be wary of an area that is overbuilt with condominiums. It could be too difficult to resell your apartment with competition from other, perhaps newer, condo communities.

That caution applies to a resort area, too, although maybe not to the same degree. You have to take the entire town into account to decide if it can support a growing number of condo complexes. Some vacation spots can, since there are always more and more second-home hunters coming along to buy. However, if you're visiting three complexes situated in a row along the highway, heed that warning.

If you plan to rent your condo apartment, you'll want to read Chapter 17 before signing any sales contract (although there is plenty about renting coming up, too, in this chapter).

Whether buying a house or condominium, take the time to drive around a town and a particular neighborhood and note day-to-day activity. Get a feel for it before you plunk down money to buy. Contact the chamber of commerce, too, and ask for brochures and other printed material about the area. That can help you decide about buying and can serve the secondary purpose of enhancing your vacations, when you finally settle in, by pointing out attractions to visit that may be new to you. Hold on to all of that material. You can use it when tenants check in (there is talk about this and other ways of helping them enjoy their stay in Chapter 17).

WORKING WITH A REALTY AGENT

By all means avail yourself of the services of a real estate agent in the community that interests you. Maybe that salesperson represents several towns in a small geographic area. You can tell by talking with him or her if that is so or if you'd be wise to speak with an agent in another community as well to see homes there.

There is usually no need to register with more than one agent in one specific resort region. A Multiple Listing Service, which will show you all homes available within that area by any number of agencies, is usually broader than countywide.

As a buyer you pay real estate agents nothing for their assistance. It's the seller who pays a commission when the house is sold. So keep in mind a truth many buyers are unaware of: The agent is employed by the seller. His or her loyalty is to the seller, who is paying 6 percent of the sales price of that home. No matter how helpful realty people are to buyers, they must put the seller first. However, an agent can be very helpful indeed and will try his or her darnedest to find just the home for you.

You might want to try a "buyer broker," who specializes in working with buyers. Services of a buyer broker can cost you nothing or you might be charged a fee of around $300, which is refunded at the closing when you purchase a home through that agent.

All of this becomes a little more complicated if you are dealing with a dual agency. Let's say your buyer broker is affiliated with ABC Realty Co. The house you like is being sold by ABC Realty, with another salesperson there as listing agent. So ABC seems to be facing in two directions, with two sets of loyalties. This happens sometimes and is perfectly legal. ABC would then be very neutral toward both buyer and seller. For you, that translates into a warning to be doubly cautious about looking after yourself throughout the transaction.

Be honest with any real estate agent about the type of property you want and what you want to pay. If you are preapproved for a mortgage, the appropriate document will show your agent just how much a lender will grant you in the form of a mortgage and will be your entrée to viewing a selection of homes for sale in the resort area that interests you. If you are not preapproved, the agent might well direct you to a lender for preapproval certification before showing you homes.

A "What" Is Going Up Next Door?

If you believe the appearance of the street that interests you could be changed—a widening, for example, that could cut into your property line or some commercial buildings constructed on vacant lots—check the master plan for that town to see how those blocks are zoned and what has so far been planned in the way of improvements. You can find that plan at the city or town hall. Reading the daily newspaper regularly can also turn up new plans and projects that could affect your investment.

You can look at places slightly above what you can pay because you may negotiate the asking price down to an amount you *can* afford. Keep in mind that in some sections of the country sellers expect an amount very close to their asking price, whereas in other areas they set an asking price that allows more "give" between seller and buyer. Ask your agent what the custom is where you are househunting.

Comparables

How will you know what to bid when you see a place you like? Ask your real estate agent to show you a book of "comparables." These are listings of homes that have recently sold with their sales prices. Asking prices won't help you at all in negotiating. A seller can *ask* any price. What is important is knowing what homes *similar to the one you are considering in a similar neighborhood* have brought sellers over the last year or two. Armed with "comps," you will be an informed buyer when the talk turns to your offer for the place you want.

LOOKING AT HOMES FOR SALE

When it's time to tour properties, drive around with the real estate agent in the agent's automobile, freeing you to look at neighborhoods and ask questions without having to concern yourself with traffic, directions and other distractions.

Try not to look at too many properties in one day. Four or five is sufficient. More than that will blur your memory about what you've seen and then it becomes difficult to weigh the advantages of one home over another.

Take a notebook with you, by all means, to jot down impressions, although the agent will no doubt give you a computer printout of each house or condominium that interests you. This printout sheet will answer most of your questions, such as asking price, size of the lot, real estate taxes, room sizes, number of baths and any special features.

Naturally, you'll look at the number of bedrooms and baths, whether there is a porch or patio, and other features you want in a vacation home. A principal one to check is storage space. This is particularly important if you plan to rent your place. You will also want to put your own gear in that room/alcove/attic/closet space so you don't have to haul everything back and forth from one year to the next.

Is there a best *time* to shop? You are likely to strike a better deal in the off-season in that community, when few househunters are looking and sellers may be starting to worry.

SPECIFICALLY CONDO

Here are six points to be certain to look for or ask about when you find a condominium apartment you want to purchase.

- Be sure to read all of the documents offered you by the seller or developer, and have a lawyer read them too.
- Remember the many covenants in any condo community, and be sure you can accept them. In particular, if you have minor children and/or pets, make certain they are allowed in the condo that interests you.
- Look over the association's financial statement with a view to seeing that there's a fund for emergencies. You don't want to spend your vacation stewing over how you are going to pay for the $1,000 assessment you were hit with for unexpected repairs to some part of the complex.
- Chart maintenance costs for the last five years to see how often they have been raised and by how much.
- Check to see whether the use of recreational amenities is included in your apartment's purchase price and maintenance fee, or if you will be billed separately for those facilities.
- If you want tenants occasionally, make certain the building or complex that interests you does not prohibit short-term rentals.

Some Detective Work

By all means check out the developer of the new community you are thinking of buying into. Talk to those who have moved there to find if there are problems and how they're resolved. The local better business bureau can tell you if any complaints have been received against that community, or indeed whether the developer has filed for bankruptcy. If a development is publicly held, ask for a copy of the annual report and recent quarterly statements.

NEW-HOME DEVELOPMENTS

Whether single-family houses or condominiums, the brand-new community can be a good buy from a money standpoint. Here are two instances:

1. In communities that are just beginning to sell and where for the most part the site is still a sea of mud, developers usually offer what are known as "preconstruction prices." These are for the first several homes, which can carry price tags 15 to 20 percent lower than prices will be once that development is "off the ground." You have first choice of sites, too, when you buy into a new community at that early stage.

    Be sure there is a clause in the sales contract for the refund of your deposit—probably 10 percent—if the project is not built. Ideally, you should be able to put that money into an escrow account until closing.
2. In new communities that are almost completely sold and where the developer wants to close out either one phase or the entire development, you can find a good buy as well on those few remaining homes. Negotiate the price the way you would with any existing house or condo because the developer is highly motivated to finish up and concentrate on the next project.

IF YOU WANT TO BE A LANDLORD

You know you will be renting out the home you buy, at least for a short time each year. Naturally, you'll want a place that tenants will find attractive and not reject in favor of someone else's home. For example, do you have to climb 14 steps to get to the front door of a particular house? Maybe you don't mind, but that could cut down on your pool of potential renters to whom it could matter a great deal. Is the house you are considering at the end of a dark, dead-end road? Tenants might worry about safety. Do you want to live w-a-y out in the woods, far from any store, gas station or sign of life? You can expect to wait until a tenant shows up who shares your taste for seclusion.

For a successful, busy renting schedule, look at homes from an investment view, considering more than just your own preferences. Think mainstream.

Less Time, Higher Taxes

Some vacation-home owners are increasingly being asked to assume additional property tax burdens to pay for school expansion and other government services in fast-growing resort communities. Utah and Vermont so far are in the forefront of mandating that part-time, seasonal owners pay higher property taxes than permanent residents.

If serious landlording appeals to you, how about having tenants year-round? Buying a two-family house could assure you a rental income 12 months a year, not just a few weeks in high season. You stay in one unit, perhaps renting it when you are not there, and your year-round tenants are in the other apartment.

Looking at a single-family house with the thought of converting it to a two-family house, perhaps even more rental units, will take some work on your part. The rental agent should be able to tell you if multi-family homes are allowed in that neighborhood or indeed on that block.

If they are not, you'll have to apply for a zoning variance for your conversion, which might or might not be granted. Ask your real estate agent for a brief history of those blocks. Has anyone else converted? Was it a hard sell to the zoning board? In resort towns where the talk is of too many people pouring in, you could find your variance denied.

Also on the conversion angle, ask the real estate salesperson or go directly to the rental office in town to learn just what a conversion might encompass. For example, you may be able to make all the changes you want inside but will be prohibited from installing a separate entrance for the renter.

WHEN YOU FIND THE PLACE YOU WANT

You are holding your breath. This house on Bayside Drive looks like . . . just what you want!

What do you do now?

Well, first don't tell your real estate agent you have found the home of your dreams, one you simply must have. Remember, if you seem en-

---

Love and Real Estate: Oil and Water

What is the number one mistake those looking for a vacation home make? According to real estate agents, it's losing one's head, in a manner of speaking. "So many people come down here and become emotionally involved with houses on the waterfront," says Fred Schien, an experienced agent, "but their appetite is for more home than they can afford." Schien sells real estate at Lake of the Ozarks, Missouri, a resort area of snaking waterways offering more than 1,300 miles of shoreline.

It is hard not to become emotional about some vacation properties. But while it would be nice to love, or at least like very much, the home you purchase, it is important to stay clear-eyed and practical about the details of any real estate transaction.

---

raptured, that translates to both agent and seller as your willingness to pay full price for the house eventually, no matter what you offer initially. You are obviously not going to let your dream slip away, they reason.

So keep your cool. Say you like the place, but then mention a few flaws. The rooms will all have to be repainted. You do not like the exterior siding. It's on a busy street. Still, maybe for the right price it could work for you. You'd like to make an offer. If it isn't accepted by the seller, well, there are always other homes, and in fact that place over on Spruce Lane seemed attractive too. (Naturally, if you really want that home, you will negotiate, which everyone understands.)

Never tell a realty salesperson, even if that is a buyer's agent, the top price you'll pay for any particular home. If asked, you might reply "Well, let's see how it goes," or "I'm not sure, there are those problems with it that I mentioned."

An agent is required by law to present any written offer to a home seller. If you raise your offer in going back and forth, do so in $1,000 increments. The negotiating process is an art, not a science. It continues, with the realty agent as intermediary, until both sides agree on a final sales figure. That, incidentally, is what a home is worth: what a willing buyer will pay and a willing seller will accept.

A seller's motivation affects your success in negotiating price. In year-round communities the seller could be highly motivated—a wife has accepted a new job, let's say, and the couple must leave as quickly as possible. But with a second home that particular impetus to settle usually does not exist. Vacation-home owners might, however, be selling to slash their expenses—a second home being the first cutback—and that could be just the motivating factor you need.

Did You Know. . .

. . . that if you are buying a leisure home with your cousin and his family, or with your closest friends, you will no doubt choose to own as tenants in common? That means each of you can will your half of the home to whomever you choose. That is unlike "joint tenants with right of survivorship," which is how most married couples own property. Another option that might actually make this simpler in practice: set up a general partnership. A lawyer in the resort community can help with details, which include which owner will act as managing partner, how one owner's selling will be handled and so forth.

WORKING WITH "FOR SALE BY OWNER" SELLERS

In real estate parlance these are known as "FSBOs." Dealing with them is a sort of do-it-yourself househunt. Negotiating for the home you want will be done without an agent as buffer.

Be very careful here when dickering over price never to insult the owners' house, let alone the owners themselves. When you are making an offer, point only to the obvious points about the house, such as its lack of adequate storage, its location next to a schoolyard, and so on. Make no comment about the owners' taste and how you will have to redo the place or remove that "eyesore" wall-to-wall carpeting. The reason for these cautions: Owners love their homes and could very easily refuse to sell you the place you want because they just don't like you or your attitude. So make nice, very nice, during price haggling and other steps to buying.

In this type of purchase, keep in mind, too, that many FSBOs are overpriced by owners who—again—might think a little too highly of their homes, and who also have not had the benefit of an agent's discussing the reality of pricing with them.

You will want legal counsel for this type of sale. Be sure you engage a real estate attorney and not someone whose specialty is another area of the law.

And another point here: Never, never make out any checks to the seller of the property. Those should be addressed to a third party, such as your lawyer or the seller's lawyer.

Do You Need a Lawyer to Buy a Home?

If you have gone through real estate transactions before, you might want to skip a lawyer and that expense. In some states, too, a closing is handled by an escrow company. However, if this is your first real estate purchase and/or you are buying your first condo and you have some trepidation about that major purchase, you might, understandably, feel it worth the expense (around $300) to have legal counsel. And, as mentioned, if you buy a "for sale by owner" home, you are likely to want a lawyer to handle details of that property transfer.

THE SALES CONTRACT

When you find the house you want and have agreed on a price with the seller, the next step is to start formal proceedings to a transfer of ownership.

First comes an earnest money check from you and a sales contract, which the agent presents to the seller. Some five to 10 days later you will be expected to follow that up with a 10 percent deposit, which might also be called the balance of earnest money. However, according to Carolyn Janik, a New England real estate agent and writer, "That amount isn't mandatory. The point of 10 percent is that sellers want something substantial so that buyers don't walk away from the sale. But that figure is negotiable."

The contract contains the details of the property being sold, such as the names of the buyer and seller, the price of the home and its address, and any other point the buyer and seller agree to include in the document. If you are buying a rental home, for example, and you want the current tenants out of the property before you take title, you can have included in the contract that "the house is to be delivered vacant."

Many contracts these days also contain common contingency clauses by buyers, such as the house's being subject to a satisfactory inspection by an inspector of your choice. Another contingency is your being able to secure a mortgage at *the exact rate and terms you want* (real estate agents usually word that clause "at the prevailing rate," but you can be more specific: "a 7.5 percent, 30-year fixed-rate loan"). Another clause, depending on where in the country your house is situated, is that it be free of termites.

You could also add this sentence: "This contract is subject to attorney review for form and content for a period of (specify time, such as five business days)." There is a lot of room for interpretation there by both you and your attorney.

Can you change your mind after you have signed a sales contract? You certainly can. Maybe the house inspection turned up problems you do not want to cope with, and so you cancel the contract (and are refunded your deposit). Perhaps you can't secure a mortgage at exactly the 7.5 percent interest rate you wanted (a reason for being so specific in the contract).

Actually, many states have a three- to five-day "cooling off" period, during which time you can rescind the sales contract without offering any reason at all. Check with the attorney general's office in the state where you are buying and ask how that law is defined there.

THE CLOSING

When what seems like reams of paperwork are completed, it's time to close the deal on the sale of your home. Sometimes that meeting is held at a real estate agent's or lawyer's office. In some parts of the country property transfers are handled by an escrow company. Although sellers sometimes choose not to attend a closing, a buyer has to be there (a power of attorney might substitute for attendance).

Settlement costs can run from a few hundred dollars to as much as 5 percent of the home loan.

At some point before the closing you will be given, either by the real estate agent or your mortgage lender, a booklet published by the government on settlement procedures and charges, based on the 1974 Real Estate Settlement and Procedures Act. This act governs most of the steps in the transfer of property and protects a homebuyer with its disclosure requirements.

Your agent will no doubt draw up a list, called a "good faith estimate," of closing costs you will be required to pay when the actual transfer of title takes place. If they haven't been paid in advance of the closing, they include fees for the mortgage application; lender's appraisal; credit report; mortgage insurance premium if you are taking out that policy; title insurance, and points if you are being charged them. You will also probably have to pay some part of the property taxes attached to the house and an amount toward a hazard insurance policy if the lender requires it. Your attorney's fee is due at the closing too.

Once you have written some checks—or handed over a money order—you will certainly feel poorer. Actually, though, in one way you are richer—you own a home.

Is the closing finished now? Carolyn Janik points out one tiny detail often overlooked: "Mention to the real estate agent before the closing to remember the garage door opener if there is one. Keys are rarely forgotten at a closing, but openers are, and they're certainly more expensive to replace."

Ah, *now* you're finished. The place is yours.

K E E P   I N   M I N D

➤ That old, but still valid, real estate formula for success with homebuying: location, location, location.

➤ The real estate agent represents the seller of the property (buyer brokers, however, work for househunters).

➤ Comparables, or "comps," will arm you with information needed to make an informed bid on a home.

➤ Don't inform your agent or the seller of the amount that represents your top offer for any particular property.

CHAPTER 17

Be a Landlord—
Rent Your Home for
Maximum Profit

Spend money for a vacation home? Certainly you'll have to, but you can also *make* money on your place. That income can be simply a bonus for having a second home, or it can be money that is truly needed to meet at least some of the expenses of your having a getaway.

So why not become a landlord and rent your place when you're not there or at least for some of the time while you're at home?

IT'S WORK

Not everyone really wants to be a landlord or would do well at it. It very definitely is a job. Even turning rentals over to an owners association or realty agency, letting them handle the whole business for you, takes not only some thought and time on your part but also mentally staying on top of your investment. Being a hands-on landlord naturally takes a lot more effort.

Still, when that rent check appears in your mail, the time and aggravation that went before is almost forgotten and forgiven. How long would it take you to earn that amount with a part-time job? In some respects, renting brings *very* easy money.

Let's see how landlording can become as painless as possible for you. And while we're at it, let's see if we can add another digit to your annual rental income.

Come Again?

One landlord told us that when he let his seaside house to a Pennsylvania couple, they spray-painted the entire row of small evergreens leading to the door.

"Why?" he asked them, aghast.

They, equally aggrieved, responded, "When we came to Maine, we expected blue spruce."

A landlord writing in *Yankee* magazine

RENTING AT THE RESORT CONDOMINIUM

If you live in a posh resort condo community, and this holds true for a few single-family home developments as well, there's likely to be a plan for those who want to rent their homes that is managed by the owners association or by the developer. If you are in this type of complex, here are some questions to ask in the administrative office that oversees rentals.

- Who exactly runs the rental program?
- Who sets the rents—that office or you?
- How much do you have to pay that office to have your apartment rented?
- Do you receive all of the rent money, less the fee, or is residents' rental income placed in a "pool" for all owners to share?
- How successful is the rental program at that community? Past performance records should be available for you to look through.
- Can you arrange your own rentals? Is there anything in the covenants that says leasing your house or apartment must go through the community association?

If you choose to have your community organization find tenants, you won't have to stir outside your building or complex and are likely to find the role of landlord rather easy as long as your place is rented when you want.

If you feel that the complex is not as successful as you would like at renting, or if you would like to try your hand at it while they're working on finding a tenant, read on.

RENTING ON YOUR OWN

When you live in a house that is not part of a community that handles rentals for owners, or you own a condominium that does not provide that service either, then you are left to your own devices to rent. Here are some tips to make the most of that do-it-yourself situation, which is, after all, more common than having a resort complex do it for you.

You might want to let a real estate agency in your community find tenants for you. That's likely to be the most practical approach unless your second home is close enough to your principal residence for you to drive back and forth to show prospective tenants your place (although you might have a friend in that community who will do it for you). Agencies will screen tenants, show them your home, handle the lease, keys, and the like.

An agency is likely to charge you from 10 to 20 percent of the rent for finding a tenant. If you want them to do any more, such as collect the rent or in any way keep an eye on your place, that's a whole other department—management, which is covered in the next chapter. Be sure you know what you can expect for just that rental fee.

If you would like to rent the place yourself, you can find tenants by advertising in the newspaper in your year-round residence and perhaps in nearby towns as well. You can also put notices in your company newsletter, religious bulletin or any other local periodical that could bring you a renter. Try the Internet, too.

You can set the rent based on what you see being charged for similar homes or apartments in your resort locale. You can discover going rates by reading the classified ads in the daily paper there and by looking in real estate offices' windows, where many agents post pictures of houses and apartments for sale and rent with the dollar amounts being asked by owners.

You might want to check your prospective tenant's creditworthiness. Look up "Credit Reporting Agencies" in the Yellow Pages, where you'll see at least a few services aimed at landlords, and advertising credit checks. These companies draw a prospective tenant's credit report from the major national reporting companies, such as TRW and Equifax, and can even track down whether your prospect has been evicted or skipped rent at a previous address. Cost: about $100 for a one-time membership, and then $7 to $50 or so for each search.

If renting yourself, when you have your place ready for tenants to move in, take some pictures of how the rooms look just before you turn the house or apartment over to the renters so you'll be able to prove damage if necessary. You'll also want to draw up an inventory sheet, listing right down to the corn-on-the-cob holders what you are leaving for your renters, so they—and you—can check that list at the end of the rental period to be sure everything is accounted for.

Check on any local rental restrictions, such as a ban on "groupers" (unrelated people, such as a group of young coworkers or college students, sharing a home). There might also be a limit on the number of people who can live in a house or apartment of a particular size that could affect whom you choose as tenants.

Try to rent for as long a period of time as possible to avoid comings and goings by a number of tenants. Many homeowners these days rent for only a full season. They accept tenants for a month or, even worse they feel, for a week if it is late in the year and no season-long tenant has appeared. You ought to at least try for the longer term first.

Calculate what a utility bill is likely to be during the time your tenant will be there and include that figure in the rent you set. You might allow local telephone calls, but ask tenants to put long-distance phoning on their credit cards. Get your rent money up front, of course. If you know your tenants, whether before their leasing or because they have returned for a second or third year, you might want to loosen up and just ask them to pay the utility bill when it comes. For those new to you, however, leave as little as possible for them to pay by themselves.

Speaking of money, your tenants will need to know whether they have automatic access to recreational facilities at your community or if they will have to pay for play.

A DIFFERENT SPIN ON RENTALS

Do you want to make even *more* money from rentals?

Let's say your vacation home is in a locale where summer is the high season. You rent your place for the month of July, earning perhaps $4,000. You and your family visit on weekends in May and June, and spend the month of August there, leaving after Labor Day.

How about renting it to just one tenant during the long off-season, particularly if you have no desire to visit then? You could have someone move in, say, October 1and then leave May 1, or whenever you specify. Maybe your month-to-month rental would bring you $650 a month or close to $5,000 for the off-season, depending on how much time you want to leave open for your own use preseason and postseason and how much you spend for repairs and maintenance. Couple that $5,000 for the off-season with your July rent, and you are doing all right—$9,000. Actually, you are doing very well indeed.

Or—and here is another possibility—you could find that $5,000 is enough for the expenses that you need a rental income to cover. You might elect to keep the house for your own use the month of July instead of finding a tenant. That gives you all summer at your getaway.

Who would rent in the off-season? Off-season leasing is a fairly common occurrence in some resorts. Is your home within commuting distance of a college or university? A student might be perfect because he or she returns home for the summer. Some folks who work year-round in the resort area are also likely to be interested in an attractive house or apartment. When they must leave—probably to return again in the fall—they stay with family or nearby friends for the summer.

None of This and None of That

If there is an owners association in your community, be sure your tenants see a copy of the covenants. And be certain they agree to abide by them. They are obliged to do so the way any permanent, full-time resident must.

Summer is used here as an example, but this can work in a winter hot spot, too, which is usually very attractive in the spring, summer and fall. Pegi and Jay Adam, for example, are avid skiers. They take advantage of every opportunity to head for their three-level, three-and-a-half bedroom condominium in Mount Snow, Vermont. In fact, they drive north from their New York City jobs every winter weekend.

"We're skiers," says Pegi Adam. "We're not tempted to go there between ski seasons." By the time April 15 rolls around, the Adam family (the couple has two children) is ready to leave Mount Snow until the next winter. And leave their place to the tenants.

Of course, a vacation home should be for your own enjoyment, as we noted in Chapter 1. If you can afford to make use of it 12 months of the year, good for you. You've made a purchase you will truly enjoy to the fullest. But if you need more income, and can bring yourself to stay away from that place a sizable chunk of the year, you can pick up some nice extra rent checks. In a way, that's enjoying your home to the fullest too, isn't it?

DO YOU NEED A LEASE?

You certainly will want one in a situation described above of a long-term, off-season rental. You will want it very clearly spelled out to your renter that he or she must move out by a specified date. You might want to add that that tenant can move back in again May 1 or September 15 or whenever you specify.

On the whole, it's surprising how many expensive vacation homes are rented by their owners with no lease. If renting without a lease makes you just a little twitchy, you can draw up a letter that you and the tenant sign spelling out the details of the rental.

Or you can pick up a standard lease form at any stationery store. Standard leases are drawn up by attorneys for building owners' groups so they favor the landlord.

Fill in every blank, even if you simply write "N/A" for "not applicable." You have the freedom here to include any restrictions you want for the tenant's stay—no pets, for example. You can also add a few lines to the effect that the tenant is responsible for mowing the lawn in the summertime and keeping the driveway and sidewalk clear of snow in the winter.

You will include in the lease, of course, the rent you are charging. If it is common in your community, you might want to add a pet deposit (if you allow those folks to bring Fido) that will be returned if Fido does no damage. If a cleaning deposit is common, write that in too.

PREPARING YOUR HOME FOR
THE TENANT HORDES

Charge a pretty penny in rent and you'll have to have your home furnished rather nicely, not with odds and ends that resemble a 1958 motel room.

In a simpler home—translation: low-rent—you can get away with, well, simpler furnishings, although here too everything must be clean and not dilapidated. Even tenants paying low-end rent will expect a comfortable, attractive home for their stay.

Every tenant, whether renting high-end or low-end properties, will expect such basic services as heat, hot water and electricity—and their *prompt* repair in case of malfunctioning. In some very warm climates, providing room air conditioners or central air-conditioning is expected too.

Dinner for Eight

Some condominium associations will make their own de-mands when renting your unit for you, such as your having the place fully stocked for eight, maybe even twelve, people. They will have a checklist of furnishings you'll have to provide from a can opener to the number of beds. Real estate agencies han-dling your rental are likely to hand you an inventory checklist to fill in and will point out gaps in your place they feel should be filled, but they will pretty much go along with what you say comes with the place.

You will also have to provide dishes, silver, pots and pans, an iron and ironing board, and other necessities for living comfortably a week or a month in a private home. Leaving sheets, towels, blankets and pil-lows for tenants may be left up to the individual landlord where you are. Just be certain tenants know whether those necessities will be in-cluded in the inventory.

There should be a table and a few chairs around it for mealtimes. Add a sofa or loveseat in the living room, or at least several easy chairs, and something on the walls—and that should be sufficient decor. Bed-rooms ought to have a good mattress and at least one bureau. These two items are the only mandatory furnishings, for you might not have room for any other furniture.

It's easy to make a vacation home look attractive to renters without spending a fortune. An arrangement of straw fans can serve as "art-work" on a wall, as can baskets and, frankly, anything you're not using in your principal residence. Mismatched wood furniture can be spray-painted the same color to give the pieces a unified look. Thrift shop sofas and side chairs, as long as they are comfortable and not threadbare and/or spouting springs, can be slipcovered with a ready-made, one-size-fits-all cover, available these days in a variety of prints for about $100. Remember, a house in even the best location can't look thrown together and/or dismal. It will either go unrented or you'll have to deduct a sizable chunk from the rental fee.

What you will *not* want in a rental home is any item of particular value to you, monetary or sentimental. These should be removed for the duration of the tenant's stay. Any personal memorabilia, such as family photographs, sports trophies and the like, should go in storage. End tables and most kitchen countertops should be clear for tenants' own belongings. Renters know they are living in someone else's home, but they don't want to see too much evidence of those owners. Remember, too, your vacationers will be bringing their own gear, which will fill your place up again in a very short time! So make those rooms as impersonal as you can, even if they look stark to you.

WHERE WILL ALL YOUR STUFF GO?

How easily can you get away from your getaway come rental time? Will you take your personal items and some furnishings back home between your stays and the tenant's rental term, or is there room at your house, building or complex for storing some gear so you don't have to go back and forth with it?

We recommended earlier that when househunting for a place you expect to rent, be certain there's plenty of storage space. Pegi Adam, who has been leasing to the same Floridians every summer for the last three years, notes: "They leave their stuff there for the winter, which is possible because we have so much closet space." So much storage room that the Adams can stash a good deal of *their* belongings in the condo all summer.

"I have large plastic containers," says Adam, "and I just pick up all the clothes and other things we want removed, including everything from the medicine cabinets. We have a locked closet on each floor for the containers. I can pack for a rental in 20 minutes. When I'm finished, it all looks like a hotel room."

If you can't keep your belongings somewhere in your home while tenants are there, perhaps you have a friend in the resort town who has extra space.

If you're getting a nice rental fee and don't want to haul a carload of sports equipment, duplicate appliances and other items back to your

How They Spend Their Many Vacation Days

If you're looking to buy with rental income in mind, consider the habits of international visitors. Since North American workers have fewer vacation days and holidays than many of their counterparts in other industrialized countries, it could increase your rental possibilities to buy at a destination that's popular with vacationers from abroad. According to figures compiled in 1993 by William M. Mercer, Inc., here are the average number of days off from work in selected countries:

Country	Legal Minimum	Typical Practice	Public Holidays
Brazil	22	22	11
Canada	10	20	11
France	25	25–30	13
Germany	18	30–33	13
Hong Kong	7	20–30	17
Japan	19	20	14
Mexico	14	15–20	19
Sweden	30	30–32	9
United Kingdom	0	25–30	9
United States	0	20	10

And of those vacationers so richly endowed in time off, the top ten states (with millions of 1994 international visitors) are:

1. California   5.2 million

2. Florida   5.1

3. New York   4.4

4. Hawaii   2.8

5. Nevada   1.9

6. Massachusetts   1.0

   Illinois   1.0

   Texas   1.0

9. Arizona   .9

10. Georgia   .6

principal residence, you can also consider renting a small self-storage unit in or near your resort community. When you return to vacation, you simply take the items out of the rental space.

NICE TOUCHES THAT CAN PAY OFF

Ideally, your first tenants are excellent, and they like your place so much they come back every year. Poof, there go your renting worries and concerns about next year's crop of renters.

You can help bring that about (you can't do anything about the luck factor in this equation) by adding a few special touches to your renting procedure.

- Leave a list for your tenants outlining how various appliances and machines work at your place. Leave another note about local trash and recyclable pickups, curfews for young people if any, and anything else you think your renters will find of community interest.
- You might spend a few hours collecting brochures about the area's points of interest and tourist attractions. Leave them on the kitchen or dining table for the tenants.
- Collect some menus from local restaurants, especially casual and take-out places. You might also add a note to the effect that "Route 16 has many of the fast-food chains. You can pick it up by taking Rosewood south to the traffic light, and then just follow the sign." Note whether the local supermarket or grocery store delivers. Is there a nearby fresh fish store? All of these tips can be a lifesaver for renters who know nothing of your community, and they do not detract at all from the renters' fun of discovering new places themselves.
- If you know your immediate neighbors, you might ask them to say "hi" to your new tenants to make them feel welcome. And allow your neighbors to unofficially keep an eye on your place while the renters are there.

All of these little extras go a long way toward ensuring that good tenants return. It is little effort for a very important payoff.

FOR MORE INFORMATION

The Landlord's Troubleshooter, by Robert Irwin (Dearborn Financial Publishing, 1994, $14.95) will help small landlords by offering solutions to dozens of problems all of those property owners eventually encounter.

Many states offer printed materials for landlords, explaining state laws and offering general information as well. Contact the consumer affairs office in the state capital where your second home is located.

KEEP IN MIND

➤ Renting once, or periodically throughout the year, will bring you an income that can offset some of your second-home expenses.

➤ Depending on your vacation style, consider renting for the entire off-season to one tenant.

➤ Tenants will expect a reasonably well-appointed house or apartment, which you can provide at a not-too-great cost.

➤ Take a few extra steps to ensure that good tenants return again and again.

CHAPTER 18

Maintaining Your Getaway When You've Gone Back Home

When you're at home and read about seven days of steady rain in your vacation community, you will be concerned.

When a friend there calls and tells you about a string of burglaries in the neighborhood, you will wonder about your home.

When you hear a message on your answering machine from your tenant asking you to call him as soon as you can, you will worry *big time*.

It *is* a responsibility, owning real estate 60 or 600 or 2600 miles away from home. If you rent your property part of the time, you'll understand the special problems of the absentee landlord.

Obviously, you'll have to arrange to have your investment looked after when you are not there. If you are in a condominium community, this is not that much of a concern. But owners of single-family or two-family homes will be looking for assistance. If that is you, you have some choices.

THE GOOD NEIGHBOR

A responsible friend or neighbor could be a blessing, especially if he or she is just a stone's throw from your vacation property. "Fred" can check for frozen pipes and look at the roof after a storm (from the ground, of course), checking for missing tiles. He can drive around periodically to be sure the place is still secured and go inside to make certain it is. He can call repair people for you and let them into and out of the house. And he can close your getaway for you after a tenant has left. Such a jewel!

Naturally, if your friend or neighbor fills this bill, you will probably sign him or her up on the spot. Payment? Understandably, it's a rare good neighbor who will do all of the above for free. After all, he or she has a life too. But you can work out an arrangement that is satisfactory to both of you.

Deborah Sullivan and her husband, Dennis Murphy, own a second home in the Dordogne section of France. The Ohio couple became friendly with their next-door neighbor, who speaks fluent English and owns a shop in the village. He became—you guessed it—the good neighbor for them.

Sullivan, a trained CPA, handles the renting, which is probably easier for her to do since the couple lease to Americans (at American dollars). But their next-door neighbor and his wife take care of other management details that go along with a rental property. They also serve as greeters for new tenants, helping them with car breakdowns, currency and sightseeing questions, and any other problem or concern. In fact, in advertising their house, the American couple add the line "the people who will receive you speak English," which can be a big plus for tourists in a part of France where not everyone does speak that foreign tongue. For their time, Sullivan and Murphy pay their neighbors 10 percent of gross rentals.

Could that work for you? Truth to tell, sometimes it does and sometimes, well, it doesn't. One couple, mentioned elsewhere in these pages, engaged a friend to look after their condo for them and, as the wife notes, "Part of the deal was she was supposed to go there every month to pick up the rent and *see the place*. But she just stood at the door and took the check. One tenant took down a freestanding fireplace, put it in a storage room and then left with the key. She was not supposed to sublet, but she did. She would skip rent, and then her checks bounced and we'd be stuck with the charges. I'd never do that again (the couple has since sold the condo). Next time I'd probably go with professional management."

If you think your friend falls more into the "jewel" category than the possibly well-meaning helper in the latter tale, do be certain to explain *exactly* what you want to avoid misunderstandings.

Some vacation-home owners prefer to leave their places in the hands of the pros.

Where IS Everybody?

The city of Boulder, Colorado, became increasingly frustrated trying to send notices to nonlocal property owners. So in 1994 the city required the owner of any rental property who did not live within the county to appoint an individual to serve as the owner's local agent. At least one property management firm sent letters to owners offering a local agent service for $75 annually.

PROFESSIONAL MANAGEMENT

First, there is a difference between a rental company and a management company, even though both might be operating under the same firm name. The rental branch of the firm finds tenants and will collect rents for you if you like (most small landlords find that aspect of rental ownership no problem, however, and just have their one or two tenants mail them the rent check each month). Also, some real estate agencies will oversee the cleaning up between tenants and find someone to mow the lawn on a regular basis. You can have tenants call them with maintenance problems, and the agent will relay that to you so you can hire plumbers, electricians or whoever else is needed. For all of that you can expect to pay 10 to 20 percent of the rent. Be certain you know exactly what services any company will provide at the rate they are charging. If it isn't listed, they don't do it.

A professional management company may handle management details for medium or large developments only and not for individual owners. However, sometimes a small-property owner is welcome to its rolls, and there are companies, too, that specialize in accounts of smaller apartment buildings and apartments in multifamily houses.

Management companies can provide a variety of services, including but not limited to those already described. For large complexes they hire personnel, prepare taxes, publish resident newsletters and more. But our concern is the small landlord. And for the small-property owner as well, professional managers can make life considerably simpler.

Pam and Bill Falwell, year-round Massachusetts residents, have engaged a service some of their neighbors use. The couple has an apartment at a 50-unit condominium in New Hampshire, which Pam Falwell says, "We are lucky enough to be able to rent all four seasons.

"The company checks the apartment every week," she says, adding that naturally that management representative will not go into a rented condo without the tenants' permission. He or she looks to see whether the place needs cleaning between tenants, that the heat is not turned up inordinately high, that tenants haven't left a log burning in the fireplace after they've checked out and other landlord-type tasks. The company then sends the Falwells a report on its findings. It could handle renting, too, but the couple prefers to do that themselves.

Another Management Style

New Yorker Peter Rothholz and his family own a vacation home in Barbados. "Management" for him is a housekeeper who keeps him posted by phone on what needs to be done around the place, how the current tenants are faring and other typical concerns of a second-home owner who is also a landlord. Rothholz feels an agent would charge more. "We're very fortunate," he says. "Our housekeeper is terrific. Plus she has a whole coterie of plumbers and electricians and other people who actually come over and get the work done."

That management fee: $25 a month. Naturally, these companies' services vary from one to another, and from one part of the country to another. You might have to pay more where you are or because you are asking for more: having the company call in repair people, for example, or overseeing some installation work.

The Falwells also own rental property at Cape Cod, which they manage themselves. They vacation at both New Hampshire and the cape and so can see the places for themselves a few times a year.

You can find a good agency by calling a few property owners for references and asking some homeowner associations whom they use. Ask the company you are considering how long it has been in business.

Does it handle a number of small landlords like you? You don't want to end up at the bottom of the "In" basket while the staff puts the concerns of its 50-, 100- or 200-unit buildings and large complexes far above yours.

CLOSING UP YOUR HOME FOR THE SEASON

Which season won't you be there?

If it's winter and you're closing your summer place, there is plenty to do to secure that home against the cold and against breaking and entering too. When you are ready to leave, whether immediately after Labor Day or after Thanksgiving dinner there:

- Shut off the water.
- If you are going to be gone for many months, you can close the place down completely or elect to pay a reduced heating bill. If you opt for the partial shutdown, set the thermostat low, around 50 degrees or perhaps lower, to keep the house from freezing.

Ask your seasonal neighbors just how much they close up and turn off when *they* leave for a long winter. A lot depends on how harsh those months are where you've been vacationing. A summer place in Georgia doesn't take the same battering from the cold that a summer place in Wisconsin does.

Consider, too, who will be looking after the place for you. You'll want to be certain someone will shovel snow and check the roof after major snowfalls, as we have discussed throughout this chapter.

When closing up a permanent home in the south and heading north to escape the steamy summer, the precautions are different:

- Give some thought to leaving on the air-conditioning or house fan while you are away but only if you'll have someone checking the house frequently. The biggest problem in these regions of the country can be mildew and dampness from high levels of humidity.
- Turn off the gas and electricity (if you are leaving the air conditioner or fan on, don't turn off the circuits for them).
- For as much circulation of air as possible, leave closet doors open.
- Protect furniture from dust and fading by covering pieces with old sheets or similar material.

- Shrubbery around the house should be kept trimmed so that a burglar cannot hide in it. Naturally, you'll need to have the lawn mowed regularly.

No matter which season your home will be closed, there are some general suggestions to ensure a proper "shutdown":

- An obvious suggestion, but still . . . be sure all doors and windows are locked. Actually, this might not be so obvious. Surveys show that 42 percent of home burglaries do not involve forcible entry, just unlocked entrances. Doors should be solid-core wood at least one and three-quarter inches thick. Hollow doors are easy to break down, and those with glass panels are better yet for the nimble intruder.
- Have mail either forwarded to you by the post office or held there, or ask a friend in your resort area to take it in for you. If you opt for the latter, leave your friend some large, stamped manila envelopes so he or she can quickly send mail on to you.
- Remove any spare keys you may have hidden around the property.
- If your vacation home will be empty while you are away, you might want to install an answering machine to your home to thwart thieves who call to see if a house is vacant.
- Stop newspaper delivery or have a friend pick up your paper if you still want to see it. Or enter a short-term subscription where you are.
- Timers can help give the appearance of someone at home if you are going to be away for just a few weeks. For a whole season—or longer—timers could look "timed" enough to give away your long absence to a burglar.
- Having a neighbor park his or her car in your driveway from time to time could also give your place that "everybody's at home" look.
- Bugs and rodents can be a problem in any closed home. To discourage these pests from invading, be sure to get rid of all food or at least make certain it is in airtight containers. Do the same with soap and candles or take them with you away from the house. Also, do not store newspapers or paper bags.
- Speaking of food, unplug and remove everything from the refrigerator, clean it thoroughly and then leave the doors open to prevent mold and mildew.

- You might want to put a screen over the chimney top to discourage pest invaders; and look to see if there are any cracks along the exterior of your home that could be another access point. Caulk any you find. More on pests: Don't forget an annual termite check, usually in the spring, if you live in an area of the country where those trouble-causing munchers are a problem.
- Finally, be sure at least one friend in your vacation area has the address and phone number where you can be reached.

HIGH-TECH HELP

If your home is expensive, you might want to—or no doubt probably will—look into high-tech security that will be in place when you aren't there. Some of these surveillance systems will not only alert authorities if someone is trying to break in, but they can also sound an alert if there is a power outage of more than a few hours. Some systems can detect flooding, an abnormally low indoor temperature, a freezer breakdown, smoke or fire. There are also devices that can monitor a furnace.

Check the Yellow Pages under "Security," and be certain to check references. Call your local consumer affairs office, too, to make certain the company you are considering engaging is solid.

ANOTHER SAFETY CHECK

It is also wise to contact the police department in your resort area to see if they have any safety guidelines for homeowners. Some will send a member of the department to a resident's home for evaluating if it is secure or burglar-friendly. That is a free service. Another service that might be commonplace in your area: police patrol of vacant homes. Ask and see if that is possible where you are.

KEEP IN MIND

➤ You will very likely need someone—amateur or professional—to keep an eye on your property when you're going to be gone for a season or more.

➤ If you're unable to line up a friend or neighbor in your resort area to take on that role, consider professional management, which can provide peace of mind for a usually reasonable fee.

➤ Security equipment is sleek and very high tech these days. You might want to look into some programs and systems that can monitor your home for safety as well as look after its mechanical and electrical systems.

CHAPTER 19

A Few Words about Taxes and Insurance

Death and taxes may be life's only certainties, but substitute insurance for the "d" word, and you have the certainties that pertain to second-home owning. We offer a few suggestions to help you get the most out of both.

1986 TAX CHANGES

Tax changes in 1986 tightened breaks considerably for those who rent out their second homes. Some deductions are still available, of course, but, as we stated earlier, a vacation home should be purchased for both enjoyment *and* long-term appreciation. You certainly want to realize a profit when you sell, but if you're looking for a strictly money-making investment, you would do well to explore areas other than a second home.

TODAY'S TAX PICTURE

We will begin with—and mention again—the fact that the Internal Revenue Code is enormously complicated in addressing vacation homes—even the U.S. Tax Court admits it is! One second-home owner said, "I've always handled our tax returns with no trouble. But the first year we had our vacation home, I couldn't do it. Had to take it outside. It really takes a specialist." So do consult your own tax advisor with any questions about tax benefits, or the lack of them, vis-à-vis your personal situation.

He Said It

"Our Constitution is in actual operation; everything appears to promise that it will last; but in this world nothing is certain but death and taxes."

Benjamin Franklin
Letter to M. Leroy [1789]

Actually, it would be smart to clarify with your accountant what awaits you in this area *before* you buy that second home. How you want the IRS to view the property will depend on how much you plan to use the getaway yourself, how heavily you want to get into renting and how much you need that income, the amount of your household income and how much you need deductions.

The following discussion should help answer some of the most commonly asked questions about second homes.

- *What constitutes a vacation place?* To qualify as a vacation home, the IRS says a home must be suitable for year-round occupancy. Minimally, that means kitchen facilities, a place to sleep and a toilet—in other words, those items and spaces that make it livable. If you have a second home far in the north with no furnace, that home might not meet the IRS test. Otherwise, for federal tax purposes your second home can be a house, condominium, cabin, manufactured home, recreational vehicle or a boat.
- *I've bought my home strictly for enjoyment. I won't rent it out, or at least not often. What is my status?* Your tax situation is simple as these things go. Your purchase is deemed "personal use" property. You can deduct mortgage interest on it the same way you do on a principal residence. Generally, you'll be allowed that interest deduction provided the mortgage loans on both your principal home and your vacation getaway do not exceed $1 million. Property taxes are deductible, too, for both homes.

If you rent your vacation home for no more than 14 days a year and during the rest of the time it is used by you or family and friends you don't charge fair market rent, or you leave it vacant, then you don't have to report rental income and naturally can't take any rental cost deductions.

- *We not only expect to visit our home for more than 14 days but also to rent it for more than 14 days.* In this case you're entitled to deductions for mortgage interest, real estate taxes and any casualty losses. Other deductions follow a complicated "mixed-use" formula, almost certainly calling for interpretation from your tax adviser.

- *I don't plan to use my second home at all or at least hardly ever. I bought to rent.* The individual purchasing a vacation property strictly for investment is not likely to be reading this book, which concentrates on the purchase of a vacation home for enjoyment, and incidentally for rental income. This type of investor is subject to still other IRS rules.

- *Are the days I spend visiting the house to work on repairs and maintenance chores considered personal use?* No, they are not even though your children are out front swimming in the lake and having a wonderful vacation during that time.

- *What about my home equity loan?* You can deduct interest on that loan of up to $100,000. It can be on your primary or secondary home.

- *I paid two points to get my mortgage. Aren't points deductible?* Yes, but for a second home they are deducted proportionally over the life of the loan. With a principal residence, they are deducted in the year they are paid.

- *Anything else deductible?* Any loss resulting from fire and natural disasters can be deducted.

- *What happens when I sell my second home?* You must pay the capital gains tax due on that sale unless you've moved in and made it your principal residence. It's wise to seek an accountant's advice when selling a vacation home, even if you have been coping with taxes yourself in the years you've owned the property.

You have no doubt heard about the "55 or older" tax break, which means that if you are 55 years old or older and are selling your primary home where you have lived for at least three of the preceding five years, you can take a one-time $125,000 exclusion from taxation when you sell.

The key words here are *primary home.* You can't take that deduction when selling a second home.

MORE SAVINGS

If you are a married couple, you are likely to buy your second home as joint tenants with the right of survivorship. That means when one party dies, his or her share of the home reverts to the surviving spouse. However, it is sometimes wiser to buy as tenants in common, which means each party can will his or her share to whomever they choose. That is done often with second marriages, for example. Talk to a lawyer or tax advisor about the special financial advantages of a "tenants in common" ownership style.

You might want to look into a qualified personal residence trust. This allows you to move your primary or secondary home—or both of them—out of your estate, transferring the present value to named family members at some predetermined future date free of estate or gift taxes. The formula contained in that move can earn you tax savings. Talk to a professional knowledgeable about trusts and estate planning.

HOMEOWNERS INSURANCE

Not only will you want to protect your second home, but if you've taken out a mortgage, your lender will insist that you show proof of insurance.

Policies for vacation homes are more costly than for a primary residences, for several reasons. These properties are often in waterfront areas that are frequently battered by storms or hurricanes and subsequent flooding. California earthquakes, Florida hurricanes, flooded riverbanks in the Midwest, plus other natural disasters around the country, can find vacation homes first in the line of fire for damage or even destruction. The result in some regions is that insurance companies have raised rates or won't insure those homes at all. For example, as a result of Florida's 1992 Hurricane Andrew, several insurers from the Sunshine State to Maine are now writing no new policies and refusing to renew existing ones in high-risk areas.

New Yorker Peter Rothholz, who owns a second home in Barbados, notes: "The companies that insure in the Caribbean have had severe losses in recent years, and of course they pass this on to everybody, not just the people who file claims."

The rental factor in second-home ownership also raises premiums. There is the damage that can be done to be considered plus the possibility of a tenant's suing the homeowner for one reason or another.

The third ingredient in the high price of second-home coverage is the fact that many of those homes are vacant for a good part of the year, which can present a different set of problems—for example, no one is there to notice potentially dangerous situations with mechanical systems or to thwart burglars. For those who have bought second homes far off the beaten track, coverage is likely to be impossible. Keep that in mind if, for instance, the home you like is 15 miles away from a firehouse.

You and your home will be considered either a "preferred" or a "standard" risk (more about those choices coming up).

FINDING A POLICY

Generally, you can expect to pay $100 to $200 a year more for your second-home policy than for your principal residence, although figures vary from one company to another and according to what each individual wants included in an insurance package. Because the average premium for a primary home is around $350, a typical second-home policy typically costs from $450 to $550 annually.

Your coverage is likely to be pretty much the same as that for your year-round home: You can be covered for personal property and liability, and you can opt for riders for special valuables you want to insure. There is coverage for such perils as hailstorms and damage from frozen pipes. But wait a minute—this isn't your *principal* home.

The Chubb Group Insurance Companies has scratched its head, said "Something's wrong here, this can be done better," and has come up with a policy especially tailored for vacation-home owners. Chubb has tried to avoid overlap between this type of policy and coverage for a principal home, a step that can save you money in annual premiums for the vacation place. For example, the company has reasoned you wouldn't need much coverage for personal belongings because most of your clothing is in your principal home. And the furnishings there are probably better than those in your second home.

Because the typical homeowners policy picks up the tab if you're forced out of your home and must stay in a motel or similar housing,

Chubb has dropped that allowance, calculating that you can probably go back to your permanent residence. The Chubb policy can chop a couple of hundred dollars from second-home rates now being quoted by other carriers. So far it's available in only eight states, although it should branch out gradually and be copied by other insurers.

In the meantime, you need coverage *now*.

It is best to choose 100 percent replacement coverage for your vacation home. To save money, you might want to go with 80 percent coverage, which will probably slice about 20 percent from your premium payments. Be sure of that figure before deciding, though. If the difference between 100 and 80 is minimal, you'll probably want to stick with the security of full coverage. Going with 80 percent replacement means you'll have to pay 20 percent of the cost in the event your home needs total rebuilding. Whether to take that chance is your call.

Approach the company that insures your principal home first. They should not only be happy to cover your vacation getaway but should also offer you a discount on the latter or a special package rate for both.

Maintenance is important because it can help you convince an insurer of your solid sense of responsibility, as shown by how well you care for your property and the fact that you have a fire and burglar alarm system. If you have someone checking your property daily, that's an extra bonus; but daily checking is probably more than you can expect a neighbor and certainly a professional property manager to do for you. The fact that your home is visible to your neighbors and is within five minutes of a firehouse is also a bonus.

Demonstrating your sense of responsibility can put your home in the "preferred" risk category, allowing you to pay a lower premium than a second-home owner whose property is considered "standard risk." A standard-risk home lacks most of the attributes noted above as showing responsibility and will cost a homeowner 15 to 25 percent more than a preferred homeowner will pay.

Also in the area of maintenance and ensuring that precautions are taken to avoid disasters, make sure your sidewalks and driveways are shoveled. Fix wobbly front steps. Check inside to be sure there is no tangled network of extension cords, that appliance cords are not frayed, that the plumbing functions properly, and the like. These precautions will help avoid damage to your home or a lawsuit from a tenant or pedestrian passing by.

If you've purchased a very old, perhaps historic, home, you might have to buy special coverage because it's unlikely an insurer is going to guarantee replacing a home's features and details virtually impossible to duplicate today.

If you're finding it particularly tough to secure coverage for your getaway, you might call the Insurance Information Institute (see "For More Information" at the end of this chapter) for suggestions about what is known as "insurer of last resort" programs. Historic-house owners in a similar fix can contact the Washington, D.C.-based National Trust for Historic Preservation at 202-673-4000 for information about coverage for historic dwellings.

Lights, Camera . . .

Take an inventory of your belongings in your second home the way you did for your primary residence. That can help your insurer and the local police department in case of a burglary. In "olden" days (five or so years ago), using a print inventory form from a stationer was the style. That's still fine, of course, but today you might want to pick up your camera or a camcorder as you walk through your place highlighting valuables and recording serial numbers.

SPECIAL COVERAGE

For what one hopes are infrequent disasters that can strike resort areas (as well as other parts of the country), there are programs outside a homeowners policy.

Earthquake coverage is not included in a standard homeowners policy, but you can buy that protection for a few hundred dollars a year— perhaps $300 for a $300,000 house.

Reimbursement for flood damage is also not covered by a homeowners policy—terrible news to many homeowners who've been flooded out of their properties. Some lenders require flood insurance for homes in certain flood areas of a community. But if you have no mortgage or live in an area where coverage for flood damage is not required by your lender (maybe because there's been no flood there in many years), you might decide to seek that protection on your own. If you've seen on TV news programs the devastation floods can cause, and the stunned faces of homeowners reporting they had no insurance, you might want to say "Sign me up for that."

The federal government's National Flood Insurance Program, administered by the Federal Emergency Management Agency (FEMA), has offered many thousands of homeowners flood insurance. If you think your second home could be in danger of flooding, contact FEMA at 800-611-6122, ext. 58, for information about coverage. The agency also offers a free booklet, *Answers to Questions About the National Flood Insurance Program*. This is a government-sponsored program, but the policy can be purchased through insurance agents.

FOR MORE INFORMATION

Check out *The Real Estate Investor's Tax Guide*, by Vern Hoven (Real Estate Education Company, 1995). This readable book will clarify confusing tax jargon and answer any questions you may have about your vacation home.

These Internal Revenue Service numbers can provide you with assistance:

- IRS tele-tax line: 800-829-4477 (in some California counties 800-829-4032); offers automated refund and recorded tax information.
- IRS tax help lines: 800-829-1040 (for the hearing impaired, 800-829-4059); you can call here to talk to a person, not a recording. If you get no response, or lines are repeatedly busy, call directory assistance for a local number.
- IRS free publications (plus audiotapes and films): 800-829-3676.

The New York City-based Insurance Information Institute, the information arm of the industry, has printed material on homeowners insurance as well as other areas of life, such as renters insurance, automobile policies and the like. You can call them at 800-942-4242 or 212-669-9200.

KEEP IN MIND

➤ Choose at the outset how you will want the IRS to consider your vacation property: personal enjoyment only, a combination of personal use plus rental, rental only.

➤ Second homes can create a complicated tax picture. Your tax advisor can offer explanations and direction, particularly important before you buy, during your first year of ownership and again when you sell.

➤ A homeowners insurance policy for a vacation place is going to cost more than you are paying for your principal home.

➤ Be sure you have enough coverage, especially for natural disasters that could strike your resort area and which are not included in the standard homeowners coverage.

CHAPTER 20

When It's Time To Sell and Move On

Well, that was fun, wasn't it? You had many great times in your vacation home and enjoyed the community and all that it had to offer. But times have changed. Perhaps the kids are now in their teens and spend vacations working. Maybe you're interested in a different kind of getaway in another part of the country or the world. Whatever the reason, you have seriously been thinking of, well, unloading your little chunk of paradise.

GO AHEAD—DO IT

If you recognize yourself in any of the above situations, then by all means sell. Financial planners say they see far too many clients hanging on to vacation-home properties long after they make full use of them, often for appearance sake. Perhaps, owners think, it will look to their friends as if they have made a mistake buying that home in that community. Or it might look as if they have fallen on hard times and need money. Some folks hang in there because a second home is seen, to them anyway, as a status symbol.

And sometimes second-home owners don't sell because they just don't want to let go of those happy memories.

Excuses, excuses. By selling when you no longer use or want your vacation home, you will free up some money for other uses, perhaps even another getaway—of a type and in a locale that is more in keeping with your present lifestyle.

Here's another point to consider. It would be wise to sell if you see prices dipping where you are by more than a routine fluctuation. Perhaps recent storms have caused growing beach erosion that is threatening your community and making would-be buyers wonder at the future of an investment there. If you see too many condo communities on the drawing board, you might want to sell your condo before they are built and it becomes almost impossible to compete with newer, perhaps fancier, models. If overbuilding looms and will be putting a strain on facilities in town, leading to higher taxes for expansion, you might want to get out before those new tax bills are passed out.

Always, always keep up with local news in your vacation locale to be sure you see what's looming for that community—the good and especially the bad. If you're not already doing so, it wouldn't be a bad idea to subscribe to the daily paper there. You'll hear the news sooner that way than if you wait until you show up in town at the beginning of the next season.

Are there any other details to consider when selling a second home compared with selling a principal residence? Let's take a look.

WHICH SEASON IS BEST FOR A SALE?

Are you tempted to cram in one last in-season vacation in your home before putting up the For Sale sign?

Try to restrain yourself. The best time to sell a vacation property is a couple of months before the high season. If you live in a beach community, for example, would-be buyers will be looking in March, April and May in order to buy and close on their new home and then enjoy the summer there. *That's* the best time for you to have your home on the market, both in terms of selling the fastest and getting the best price.

The second best time is during the season itself, when you will certainly have a ready pool of would-be buyers in the hordes of vacationers in or near your home. If you don't want to sell then because you'll be there and don't want the nuisance of prospects passing through, you might want to rethink that position. Folks living in, and enjoying, a house make an attractive setting for househunters, one far more appealing than a dark and deserted home out of season.

If you sell very much beyond the close of the season, you more than likely will have to settle for a lower price. As your beach home remains unsold through the slow winter months, it becomes a little dog-eared and, by the time the next season rolls around, looks downright tired. To real estate agents *and* prospective buyers.

Winter resort communities can be very appealing in the summer, of course, which is really the low season for them. What might be lacking during those warm-weather months, though, is a large pool of prospective buyers, like the crowd that hits town in the high season. To some extent then, all of the above in-season/off-season suggestions apply to you skiers, too, although not as much as to those with beach community houses to sell.

Country-home owners probably consider summer the high season, with fall very attractive too. Winter, unless there are resorts and winter sports or some major sightseeing attractions nearby, is off-season (selling a rural home in the north buried under a foot of snow is certainly a challenge one wouldn't want to undertake twice).

You no doubt know down to the exact weeks how the seasons rank where you are when it comes to househunting.

Does all of this sound vaguely familiar? It is, of course, the exact reverse of the suggestions made earlier in this book on when to *buy*. Remember, we said the best bargains were to be had in the off-season where you were hunting. Now that you're selling, you don't want to be offering one of those bargains, do you?

So go with a preseason or in-season listing if at all possible. You may well be able to add more cash to your billfold for that sacrifice.

SOME HOMEWORK

You know the saying that preparation accounts for 90 percent of the success of many jobs? It's that or nearly so in selling a second home too. Keep in mind that only you know exactly how much your home has to offer any buyer, so it is up to you to call attention to its many assets and those of the community as well. You'll be selling your home's fine qualities not only to likely buyers but also to real estate salespersons.

It's also up to you to prepare your home to be shown looking its best.

There is also paperwork you will need to go through and get together before taking the next step toward selling.

12 "Musts" before Selling Your Vacation Home

1. Repair any damage to the exterior caused by sun, wind, rain and the like. If it needs it, paint or retouch the outside too.

2. Be sure the entryway is attractive. Buy new plantings and paint the front door if necessary.

3. Wash windows and make certain shades/curtains are in good condition. Every would-be buyer will go to the windows to check the view.

4. Make sure the house is clean. Dirt, real estate agents say, is the second-biggest turnoff to a sale (next to price).

5. If you're selling your home furnished, replace worn toss pillows, chipped dishes and the like. Prospects *will* notice below-par furnishings and base their offer accordingly.

6. Clean out and straighten closets, even the "junk" closet. No space is off limits to househunters opening closet and cabinet doors and drawers.

7. Repaint walls and woodwork if necessary in a neutral color.

8. Be sure all light switches work.

9. Check the plumbing. Fix any problems yourself, or call in a plumber. One tiny drip from a faucet and/or low water pressure can cause a would-be buyer to wonder about your entire plumbing system.

10. Clear off kitchen counters, leaving just flowers or a plant and perhaps some cookbooks showing. You're trying for the illusion of space, so hide appliances and other gadgets for the time being.

11. If you're selling in-season while you are staying there, take down swimsuits and towels from railings, remove ski gear from the hallway and put away other evidence of your vacation that gets in the way of the house's clean look. Yes, buyers will put *their* swimsuits on the railings, but they don't want to see *your* seasonal clutter in full view.

12. Take up cots and sleeping bags when would-be buyers come visiting. It's nice to know your little mountain cabin can sleep 12, but buyers don't want to see those arrangements. They make the house look crowded, a condition that, like dirt, you want to avoid in the context of your place.

If you live in a community with an owners association, check to see if there are any restrictions on your sale. In a cooperative, for example, buyers have to be approved by its board of directors.

Read the documents, too, for other points that will be of interest to a buyer and may advance your sale. Does a dock slip come with your home, for example? Do you have access to a free beach? Does your condo unit come with discounted ski lift tickets? Are they for prime winter weeks or for secondary ones? Is there a lively social program at your condo's clubhouse?

What does the association say about pets? You'll want to apprise househunters of that ruling. And about rentals too—whether they are permitted and for how long. Condominiums, for example, usually do not allow short-term rentals.

Will you be selling your place furnished or unfurnished? Beach and country houses are usually unfurnished, whereas ski houses as a rule come with furnishings. Condo apartments are sold either way.

Make a note to give a copy of your association's covenants—what residents can and cannot do—to the real estate agent you engage and be sure a buyer seriously considering your property sees them before making an offer.

In communities where there are obviously restrictions of some type, the agent will ask for the covenants or—more likely—will have a copy in his or her office files. But some communities are small and seem rather low-key, and no one thinks to ask about the various "no-no's" attached to living there. They can come as a very unwelcome surprise to a buyer who moves in, in the dark, and then, thwarted from doing one thing or another, turns in anger to the real estate agent *and to you.* It's far better to be prepared and to anticipate likely questions or trouble spots.

Be sure to save any receipts for repairs or replacements you make to the house preparing to put it on the market. You might need them come tax time.

Here's an idea. Draw up a simple brochure, either by hand or on a computer, perhaps on 8½" × 11" paper folded in thirds, describing your home. You can paste a copy of a photo of the place and call the brochure something like "What We've Enjoyed about This House." The brochure should list the address of the home; show a map directing a househunter to it if you feel that is necessary; describe the house in terms of lot size, exterior, square footage, number of rooms and baths and any other features likely to interest a buyer, such as a fireplace, skylight, porch, garage, parking spaces and the like. Note the property taxes, whether there is a community association and the amount of annual dues. And, of course, list any amenities that go along with the house (free admission to a nearby golf course, seasonal beach tickets and the like).

Then add a few paragraphs about the fun you've had in that house and town. You might say: "We're just a ten-minute walk to the Ice Cream Palace on Main Street"; or "Every Friday evening in season we walk to the bandshell in the park for the free pops concert"; or "The McCleery farm, two miles down RR 4, offers 30-minute hayrides around the area for $3.50 per person. Our guests, both kids and grown-ups, love them." Or maybe: "We've spent many happy hours on the porch at night, just gabbing and greeting passers-by—and digging into sausage pizza delivered from Vinnie's on Harbor Street."

One paragraph in that vein is enough. What you are doing here, as you can see, is helping potential buyers see themselves living in your home, enjoying their vacation time.

Put your name and main home phone number on the back of the brochure. Make photocopies, leaving a batch on the kitchen counter when you leave to return to your primary home and taking some with you. You can use them to do some marketing back home (more about that later).

Looking to Your Resort for Assistance

If you live in a community that offers help with selling your place, be sure you understand what that will entail and what it will cost you. Many complexes offer a sales office as one of the benefits of buying there.

SELL IT YOURSELF?

No one *wants* to pay a real estate agent's commission, and indeed more and more homeowners are doing the selling themselves these days. Should *you?*

You can try. A 6 percent commission (the typical figure) on a $100,000 house comes to $6,000. That saving might certainly make you want to put on the hat of salesperson.

This can work if you live within a two-hour or so ride to your vacation home and can drive there to show the property when someone calls. It can work if you live a greater distance away but are able to leave the showing of the home in the hands of a capable friend, who will have answers ready for prospective buyers and in general act as your "agent," although you will no doubt talk by phone, sometimes often, with the eventual buyer. You will probably want to pay your friend a percentage of the sales price of the home or perhaps a flat fee. Whatever that amount is, it will certainly be far less than what you would have to pay a realty salesperson. Do you know someone who can act in that capacity for you?

Don't spend too much time trying to sell your second home yourself, however. You could waste a whole high season. Give it a six-week trial, and if you are having no luck at all and are eager to sell as quickly as possible, then head for a realty office.

Keep your asking price reasonable and in line with others in your neighborhood. The FSBO (for sale by owner) house is often overpriced, which can lead to its spending a long time on the market. With these homes, too, many would-be buyers come prepared to haggle *a lot*, saying "Well, after all, you're saving an agency commission."

More than one FSBO homeowner has had to reduce the selling price, pay perhaps $100 a week to advertise the home in the local paper (three months, as you can see, can run $1,200), and then pay another low four-figure amount in closing costs. Keep in mind that selling the property yourself will likely save you money, but selling still *costs*, sometimes more than you calculated.

You can sell the home yourself with ads in the local newspaper there, referring prospects to you in your year-round home. You can also advertise in the newspaper of the largest city or cities near your principal residence. Advertise in newsletters and bulletins of organizations to which you belong, which can be as varied as religious groups, alumni associations or professional and hobby clubs. You can take it online too. Keep photocopying your brochure as you run out of copies. Offer to send one to anyone who shows interest in your place.

If your home is especially distinctive and in a place everyone would like, such as Hawaii or London, you might want to advertise in such national publications as *USA Today*, the *New York Times* or the *Wall Street Journal*.

GO WITH A PROFESSIONAL?

Many folks prefer to leave the whole selling business in the hands of a real estate salesperson.

You can find a good agent by asking among your friends in the vacation community and noticing advertisements in the local paper and For Sale signs on area homes. Who seems to be busy selling? Who just won an award? Who was just inducted into the Million Dollar Sales Club? Take a walk along the main street in town, look at real estate offices and the pictures they often tape in their windows of homes that office has listed for sale. You can get names that way too. Try to engage a person who works full-time and sells homes in your price range.

Interview three agents. Ask them how they would price your home and how they would market it (ads, open houses or other). An agent should not suggest an inflated sales price just to get your listing (you'll *know* when a figure sounds just *too* good).

Ask to see comparables, the books real estate offices keep of the actual prices at which homes in the community sold, so that you can note what prices places like yours in your immediate neighborhood are bringing. Comparables will help you price your home fairly. Remember, an overpriced property is the principal turnoff to buyers.

Did You Know. . .

. . . that practices for sellers' determining sales prices vary around the country? In some parts of the nation, sellers set an asking price at or very close to what they expect to receive and are insulted by haggling. In other regions—the Northeast, for one—asking prices take into account a negotiating leeway of $10,000 or more. Keep that in mind if you're selling several states away from your main home. You will want to ask your real estate agent what the practice is in your vacation-home state.

An agent can help your serious buyer find financing, something you might not want or be able to do on your own.

Try for a clause in your contract that states if you send a buyer to the agent because of your advertising or talking about the property, you pay a commission of less than 6 percent.

Don't bargain too much over an agency commission, other than making an allowance for your sending in a buyer. Human nature being what it is, agents are going to work harder for properties that will bring them as much commission as possible, and you might find your property taking a back seat to those that have been signed at the full 6 percent.

You might want to consider an exclusive agency listing—one agency will colist with other agencies but the sale goes to it and it gets half the commission; you will also have stipulated that you reserve the right to sell the property yourself.

With telephone, faxes and e-mail, you and your agent can be in constant communication, no matter how great the distance.

Here's how Rachael and Jesse Halpern handled the sale of their two-bedroom, two-bath unfurnished condo in Colorado from the East Coast. From their main home there Rachael called agents in that Colorado community (she had dealt with some of them in renting the property over the years) and picked one. The Halperns signed a contract that gave the agent power of attorney for the couple at the closing. They never spoke with the buyer, did not have to fly back for the closing and did not engage a lawyer for any part of the transaction. "We found a very reliable fellow [the realty agent] to represent us," Rachael recalls, "and everything went just fine." Indeed it did—the house sold in one week! Cash outlay for getting the place in shape? The couple paid a friend in Colorado $75 to engage a painter for some touch-ups.

FOR MORE INFORMATION

The For Sale by Owner Kit, 2d edition, by Robert Irwin, Dearborn Financial Publishing Co., 1995, $15.95. This book can help if you elect to go the FSBO route. You can learn about negotiating a sales price, helping buyers with financing and a host of other topics to assist the do-it-yourselfer.

KEEP IN MIND

➤ Sell your vacation home if you are not using it or successfully renting it often, and free up that money—perhaps for a new second home more in keeping with your present lifestyle.

➤ Just before the high season where your vacation home is located is the best time to hang up the For Sale sign; the next best is during the high season.

➤ Get appropriate papers together (covenants, special easements or restrictions, property tax statements, etc.) for your real estate agent and prospective buyers.

➤ Decide whether selling your second home yourself will work for you or whether you had better go with a realty office. If you're doing it yourself, try it only for a brief period.

INDEX

New
CD-ROM Money Maker Kits from Dearborn Multimedia

Book & CD-ROM Set

A DEARBORN MONEY MAKER KIT

THE MORTGAGE KIT
THIRD EDITION

- SELECT THE RIGHT LOAN
- NEGOTIATE THE BEST TERMS
- LOCK IN THE LOWEST RATE
- UNDERSTAND ALL YOUR OPTIONS

THOMAS C. STEINMETZ
PHILLIP WHITT

Features:

- *25 minute video help with the author*
- *12-28 interactive printable forms per CD-ROM*
- *On-Line glossary of terms*
- *Quick-start video tutorial*
- *Interactive printable book on CD-ROM*
  (Print out sections you like for closer reading or writing notes.)

Start Enjoying Greater Financial Freedom
Triple Your Investment Portfolio
SAVE Thousands on Real Estate as a Buyer or Seller

Successfully Start & Manage a **NEW** Business